Quilts from Grandmother's Garden

A FRESH LOOK AT ENGLISH PAPER PIECING

Jaynette Huff

Martingale®
& COMPANY

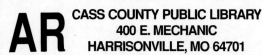

Quilts from Grandmother's Garden:
A Fresh Look at English Paper Piecing
© 2005 by Jaynette Huff

That Patchwork Place® is an imprint
of Martingale & Company®.

Martingale & Company
20205 144th Avenue NE
Woodinville, WA 98072-8478 USA
www.martingale-pub.com

Printed in China
10 09   8 7 6 5 4

MISSION STATEMENT

*Dedicated to providing quality products
and service to inspire creativity.*

CREDITS

President: Nancy J. Martin

CEO: Daniel J. Martin

VP and General Manager: Tom Wierzbicki

Publisher: Jane Hamada

Editorial Director: Mary V. Green

Managing Editor: Tina Cook

Technical Editor: Erana Bumbardatore

Copy Editor: Sheila Chapman Ryan

Design Director: Stan Green

Illustrator: Laurel Strand

Cover and Text Designer: Regina Girard

Photographer: Brent Kane

Library of Congress Cataloging-in-Publication Data
Huff, Jaynette.
    Quilts from grandmother's garden : a fresh look at
English paper piecing / Jaynette Huff.
        p. cm.
    ISBN 978-1-56477-642-6
    1. Quilting—Patterns. 2. Patchwork—Patterns.
3. Flowers in art. I. Title.
    TT835.H796 2005
    746.46'041—dc22
                                    2005018348

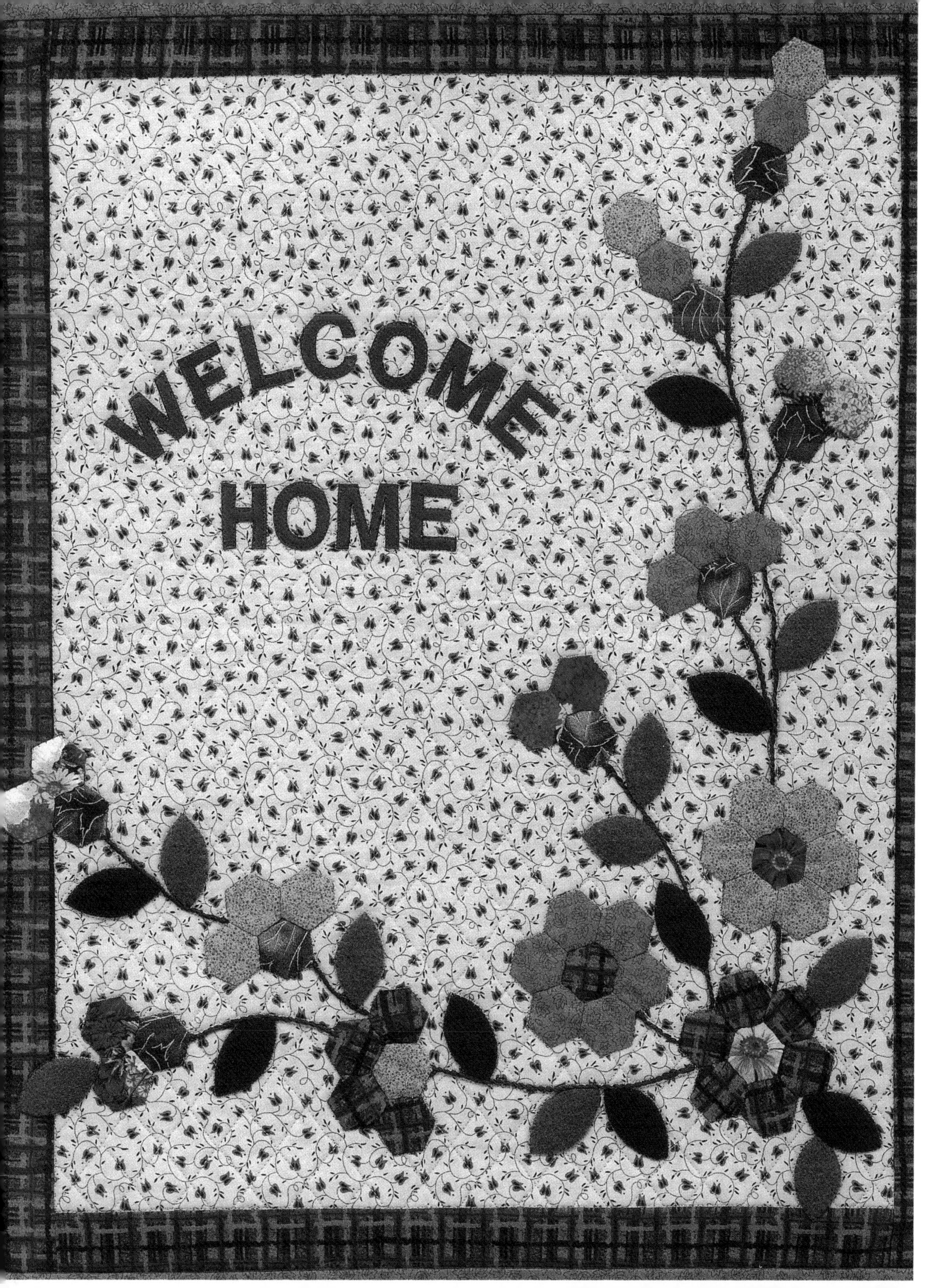
WELCOME
HOME

Dedication

To three generations of my family:

First, to my grandmother, Velma C. Parker, a professional florist for more than 50 years.

Second, to my mother, Ida Mae Borders, who loved yellow roses and taught floral design and decoration.

Third, to my sister, Martha Beth Palmer, a former florist who helped me with these designs by basting hundreds of ¼" hexagons!

These three people represent a continuous line of women greatly influenced by the beauty of flowers and the love of one generation for another.

Acknowledgments

A very special thank-you to:

The women of my miniature quiltmaking group, the Mini-Makers, who inspire and push me to make "just one more."

My publisher, Martingale & Company, and especially Mary Green, for continuing to let me share my love of quilting with others. I am truly grateful for the professional guidance and encouragement I have received.

Those quilters who support my quilt-related efforts. May all your quilted floral arrangements be beautiful!

And always, to Larry, my husband and friend, who supports all my endeavors with love, patience, and an appreciation for my quilting passion. I love you.

Contents

Introduction

Flowers have always been a source of great beauty and pleasure, and people have always enjoyed "saying it with flowers." But fresh flowers often are short-lived and gone long before we'd like. *Fabric* floral arrangements, however, can provide pleasure and enjoyment for many years to come.

Quilts from Grandmother's Garden presents a collection of floral arrangements, ranging from a simple, stylized design (see "Topiary Rose" on page 63) to a more involved basket full of color, line, and texture (see "Grandmother's Flower Garden" on page 52). There's a pattern just right for you to choose, assemble, and arrange—whatever your skill level or desire.

Take a walk with me through Grandmother's garden. Pick a few flowers along the way, arrange them into these beautiful floral wall quilts, and enjoy!

Jaynette Huff

Welcome to English Paper Piecing

English paper piecing is an easy and extremely accurate hand-piecing technique that uses paper templates as foundations to create geometric shapes such as diamonds, triangles, and hexagons. Basically, a paper template is placed in the center of a larger fabric patch. The seam allowances are folded over the edges of the paper template and basted down. The prepared fabric-covered shapes are then sewn together along their edges to create intricate geometric designs.

Grandmother's Flower Garden, one of quilting's oldest and most frequently sewn quilt designs, is made using the English-paper-piecing technique. It's a design based on the hexagon, a six-sided polygon. The hexagons used in these quilts generally have sides that measure 1" to 2".

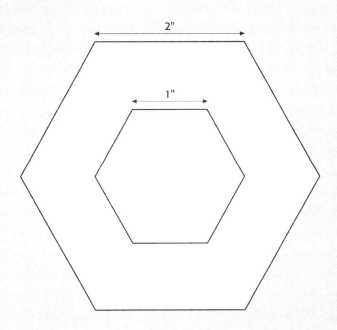

Traditionally the entire surface of the quilt is composed of these hexagon shapes sewn side by side.

A vintage quilt from the author's collection

The fabric floral arrangements included in *Quilts from Grandmother's Garden* are created using a single shape: the hexagon. We use the traditional English-paper-piecing technique as a base to create individual floral-design units (flowers, baskets, vases, and so on), which are then arranged into lovely floral pieces. However, I've tweaked the traditional approach so that rather than piece the background, as you do in traditional quilts, we appliqué these floral units onto the background fabric, leaving large open areas for you to quilt and embellish. Also, instead of the 1" and 2" templates that were traditionally used, we use smaller paper templates—just ¼" and ½" on a hexagon side—for our foundations.

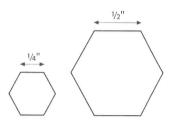

½"

¼"

DESIGNER ALERT
Any of the designs presented in this book could be made into larger quilts simply by using larger hexagons. Just remember to purchase greater amounts of fabric.

My hope is that *Quilts from Grandmother's Garden* will serve as a reference guide in addition to being a project book. My goal is to present some attractive and imaginative ways to use small hexagonal floral designs, to be a source of inspiration for everyone from beginning to advanced quilters, to help you create quilts that you'll enjoy for many years to come, and to allow you to say it with *fabric* flowers. This book provides everything you will need to know to make beautiful paper-pieced quilts, including suggestions for choosing your fabrics, creating the floral units, and arranging those units into pleasing floral designs. Keeping those quilters new to English paper piecing in mind, I've included detailed diagrams, step-by-step instructions, and color photographs for each design. With this material by your side, you'll be able to plan and create the quilted floral arrangements you've been dreaming of. Let's begin.

Elements of Floral Design

When creating floral arrangements from either plants or fabric, there are four basic design elements to consider:

1. **Line materials.** These are used to create the basic framework or outline of the design. For our purposes, fabric stems and vines are the line materials that give our arrangements their skeleton. We add our flowers, leaves, and accessories around these stems and vines. When considering the lines of your arrangement, ask yourself whether it will be tall, short, wide, narrow, curved, and so on. You'll use these lines to draw the viewer's eyes through the design and make the design suitable for different locations and uses. See the illustrations below.

2. **Primary focal materials.** These consist of the main flowers and foliage that capture our eye and provide interest and focus. These materials are usually made in the arrangement's dominant colors and are placed in central positions. They provide the main focus of our arrangements.

3. **Secondary materials.** These are smaller flowers and leaves added to complement the focal materials. They continue and emphasize what was established by the first two elements by enhancing the overall line design and balancing the primary flowers. In our quilted arrangements they are often the containers and accessory pieces (baskets, vases, bows, and so on) in addition to the smaller flowers and leaves.

4. **Filler materials.** These serve to cover up the mechanics of our work. Their job is to add tiny bits of interest, to add color to our arrangements, and to fill in any bare areas. The smallest leaves, tendrils, and berry clusters are frequently used as filler.

All four of these elements need to be present in each of our floral designs to provide a pleasing balance between the flowers, foliage, container, filler, background, and borders.

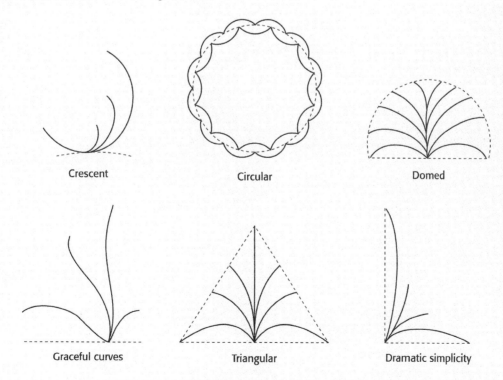

Crescent   Circular   Domed

Graceful curves   Triangular   Dramatic simplicity

Choosing Your Floral Materials

No floral designer can create beautiful arrangements without good tools and materials. Fabric floral designers are no exception to this rule.

TOOLS AND EQUIPMENT

Having good tools and using them correctly will help to ensure that you'll end up with pleasing floral arrangements. Good tools make the job of preparing and arranging the flowers, foliage, accessories, and surrounding areas more enjoyable. The following tools and equipment are recommended for your fabric floral design toolbox.

Thread. I use leftover thread of all types for basting, 100%-cotton thread for sewing, and either cotton or silk thread for appliqué.

Scissors. I recommend embroidery scissors with 4"–5" blades for cutting out fabric hexagons and for removing the fabric behind your sewn hexagons.

Paper templates. I use, and strongly recommend, commercially available, die-cut paper templates. (See "Resources" on page 79.) If you want to make your own templates, follow the directions on page 12.

Sewing pins. I use IBC silk pins with glass heads because they are thinner and longer than regular sewing pins. Pins are used to mark center points and hold appliqué units in place for basting.

Marking pens and pencils. Water-soluble, fine-line markers or fine-lead pencils are used for tracing pattern lines and marking positions. Permanent fabric markers (such as Pigma pens) are used for lettering.

Sewing machine.

Needles. You'll need hand-appliqué (size 10, 11, or 12), quilting (size 10, 11, or 12), and machine-sewing needles.

Embellishments. Buttons, beads, ribbons, and other decorative accents are frequently added to the quilts.

Iron and ironing board or ironing pad.

Rotary-cutting mat, ruler, and cutter. Used for cutting border strips.

Tweezers. Use to remove small or hard-to-reach paper templates.

CHOOSING A COLOR SCHEME

When planning your fabric floral arrangement and choosing the colors you wish to use, consider these questions:

- What time of the year or season will your arrangement be displayed (spring, fall, Christmas, Mother's Day)?
- In what setting or location are you planning to display your arrangement (casual, formal, over the fireplace mantle)?
- Who is the proposed recipient of the arrangement (man, woman, child)?
- What flowers are you representing (roses, sunflowers, irises)?
- What containers or accessories do you wish to use (baskets, vases, bows)?
- What special occasion are you designing for (wedding, homecoming, birthday)?
- What fabrics do you have on hand, and what colors do you wish to use?

The answers to these questions will help determine your dominant color choice. Once this choice is made, select other colors that complement the dominant color and add interest, pizzazz, and balance.

FABRIC SELECTION

The plant materials, accessories, backgrounds, and borders of all the quilts in this book were made with good-quality, 100%-cotton fabrics. (Specialty fabrics were only used where specifically indicated in the text.) I recommend that you prewash your fabrics so they are colorfast and preshrunk.

Plant Materials—Flowers and Foliage

Your fabric options for these projects are endless and can vary depending on how realistic, abstract, or stylized you want your flowers to appear. Here are some suggestions based on the quilts in this book.

- If a particular flower is being created, such as a yellow sunflower, select fabric prints that closely represent the real flower. (See "Sunflower Bouquet" on page 58.)

- Select the outer-border fabric first to serve as a theme print. (I frequently use a floral or landscape print.) Then choose companion fabrics that work well with the border, such as a fabric in a matching shade of green for foliage or flower colors that coordinate with those in the border. (See "Friendship Basket of Buttons and Blooms" on page 47.)

- Consider fussy cutting small flower prints that fit within the finished hexagons used to make your floral units. (See "Bow-Tied Bundle" on page 39.)

- Start with a fabric that speaks to you, and go from there. See the lovely floral border print used in "Blessed Friendship" on page 35. I loved this fabric, and I chose all the other fabrics in the quilt based around it.

- For a textural effect, use specialty fabrics such as Ultrasuede or felted wool for leaves and letters. They are easy to use and add great texture and dimension. Refer to the manufacturer's directions when using specialty fabrics; some care in preparation may be necessary, but it will be well worth the effort. (See "Welcome Home" on page 67.)

Accessory Pieces

Accessories are the nonplant items used within or alongside a floral arrangement. They include containers (vases, baskets, and planters), bows, butterflies, and so on, and are added to complete an arrangement or design. Consider the following when creating your accessory pieces:

- Choose a container with the right color and shape to enhance the overall design and balance your flowers. For instance, to create a tall arrangement, use a tall vertical vase. (See "Sunflower Bouquet" on page 58.) To create a more circular look, a low, wide container would work best. (See "A Spring Basket from Grandmother's Garden" on page 32.)

- Choose what looks natural for your floral accessories. In terms of fabric selection, often a "real" or natural-looking color or print works well (such as a basket-weave print for a basket). Such prints will serve to complement the arrangement, but won't take the focus away from the flowers.

- Add some spark. Accessory items often call for fabrics that will add interest and a bit of sparkle to the arrangement; try using something different, unique, or unexpected. (See the butterflies in "Cattails and Butterflies" on page 43, or the bow in "Bow-Tied Bundle" on page 39.)

EMBELLISHMENTS

Use specialty buttons, charms, silk ribbons, and beads to add extra interest and whimsy to a piece. These types of embellishments can help to carry out the floral setting or theme, as well as add dimension and texture. Look for buttons or charms shaped like ladybugs, honeybees, snails, and butterflies; or use seed beads, jingle bells, or other embellishments that will enhance your floral designs. (See the seed-bead berry clusters on "Bow-Tied Bundle" on page 39.) Use embellishments to help you create that perfect fabric floral arrangement.

English Paper Piecing Miniature Hexagons

Now that you've gathered all the necessary tools, equipment, and materials, you're ready to start assembling your first quilted floral arrangement. The step-by-step technique is the same for all the floral units; only the number of fabric-covered patches changes.

SELECT A FLORAL PATTERN

Use the individual floral and accessory patterns shown in "Floral-Unit Assembly Diagrams" (pages 75–76) to create your own floral designs, or choose one of the complete floral arrangements from the projects in this book (pages 32–74).

We'll use this simple six-petaled flower as an example:

SELECT A PAPER-TEMPLATE SIZE (¼" OR ½")

These hexagon shapes are drawn full size and *don't include any seam allowances.* They are the finished size of your patches. You will need a paper template for each patch in your floral design. For best results, I strongly recommend that you use commercially available, precut paper templates. (See "Resources" on page 79.) These templates are made of heavyweight paper and are die-cut for greatest accuracy.

However, if you're drawing your own templates, use index cards; templates cut from this weight of paper will hold their edges and corners more accurately than templates made from standard typing or freezer paper. Using either the ¼" or ½" hexagon template (see page 8), use a light box or other light source to carefully trace the number of hexagons needed onto the index cards. It is critical that you draw and cut your paper templates accurately. Remember, you are cutting your templates to your desired finished size, without seam allowances.

SELECT AND CUT YOUR FABRICS

Choose fabrics for each design unit in your arrangement (all the leaves, petals, flower centers, containers, and so on) and cut out your fabric patches *with* seam allowances added around all six sides. Keep in mind that the precise cutting of fabric patches isn't critical with English paper piecing because the edges are simply folded over the template and basted in place. Do allow a generous ⅛" to a scant ¼" seam allowance for easier handling, though.

Below you'll find three different cutting methods you can try. Experiment with each one, and then use whichever one works best for you.

Method 1. On the wrong side of each fabric, trace the template shape using a fabric marker that you can see clearly but which doesn't show through the fabric. Be sure to leave about ½" between the shapes for seam allowances. Then cut out the fabric patches, adding a generous ⅛" to a scant ¼" seam allowance all the way around each hexagon. This method is recommended for beginners.

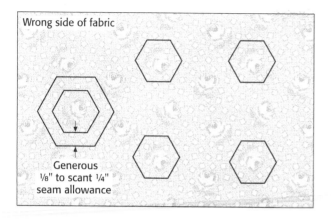

Wrong side of fabric

Generous ⅛" to scant ¼" seam allowance

Method 2. Simply hold a paper template in place on the wrong side of the fabric and trim around the template, adding a generous ⅛" to a scant ¼" seam allowance around all six sides.

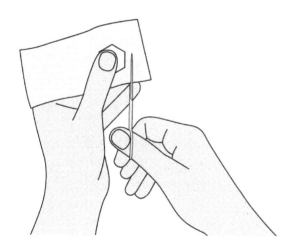

Method 3. To cut out your fabric patches faster, cut several fabric strips ½" wider than your selected templates and layer two or three strips together. Place a template on top, hold it in your hand, and carefully trim around each edge, adding a generous ⅛" to a scant ¼" seam allowance all around.

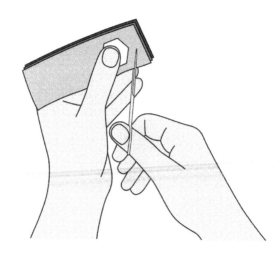

BASTE AROUND YOUR TEMPLATES

Using a needle (I prefer a size 10 or 12 quilting or appliqué needle) and a 20"- to 30"-long single strand of thread, thread the needle and knot the threaded end. Center a paper template on the wrong side of a fabric patch. Carefully fold the fabric seam allowance over one edge and finger press it in place. Hold the template in place; make sure the fabric fold is precisely at the edge of the paper template.

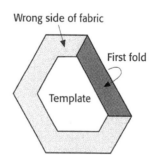

Wrong side of fabric

First fold

Template

Baste the folded-over seam allowance in place with a running stitch. Insert the needle from the front side of the patch to the back. Go through all layers (fabric, paper template, seam allowance). Each side of the smaller hexagons can be basted in place with just one stitch; larger hexagons may require several running stitches per side. Stop stitching as you near the end of the edge you're basting.

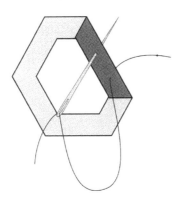

Carefully turn the fabric and template so the next edge is in position to be basted. Fold over the seam allowance of the next edge, again keeping the fabric fold close to the template edge and creating a crisp, precise corner. Come up through the folded corner of the fabric, where the two edges meet, to baste more securely. Baste this next side exactly as you did the first one.

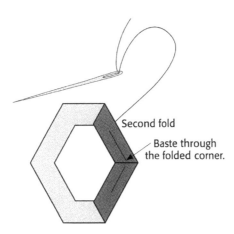

Second fold

Baste through the folded corner.

Continue around the hexagon until all the sides are basted. On the last side (the sixth fold), take two stitches. Then take a few extra stitches across the patch, if necessary, to secure any loose edges. Bring the needle out through the front of the patch and trim

the thread so there's a ½"-long tail. *Do not knot the thread.* You'll remove this basting thread later.

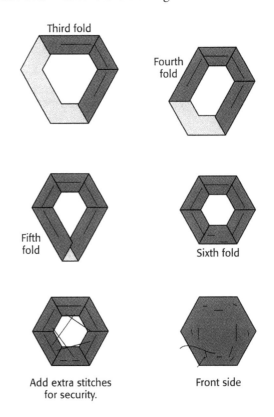

Third fold

Fourth fold

Fifth fold

Sixth fold

Add extra stitches for security.

Front side

JOIN YOUR FABRIC-COVERED PATCHES

Red Alert: This method of joining patches is different from traditional English paper piecing, so be sure to read the directions carefully, *especially* if you've used the traditional method before. This is the step where you will see your floral patterns begin to emerge, and for best results, it's important that you follow the directions carefully and join your hexagons accurately.

First, choose a center hexagon, if the unit you're making has one, and a neighboring hexagon. With wrong sides facing you, hold the hexagon edges to be joined side by side, being careful to align the edges and corners exactly. Note that the hexagons are held *flat,* not with right sides together, as in traditional English paper piecing.

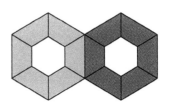

Choose a thread that matches the fabrics being joined (or a neutral-colored thread, such as a taupe, beige, or tan) and a fairly small needle, such as a quilting or appliqué needle (size 10, 11, or 12). Insert the needle under one folded seam allowance, bring it out through the corner of the fabric, and insert it into the corresponding corner of the other fabric-covered hexagon. This allows the knot to be hidden in the fabric fold. Pull the thread until the two corners are aligned.

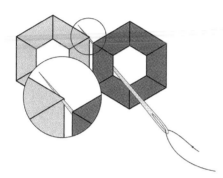

From the back side of the patches, use a flat, straight stitch (see page 23) to sew back and forth across the two edges. Be sure to catch only the edges of the seam allowances, not the paper template.

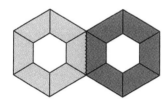

Continue along the side until you reach the other corner, making sure that your stitches are tight and secure and that the corners of the hexagons line up. When you reach the end of the side, take an extra stitch or two and knot the thread.

If you're adding another adjacent hexagon, match up corresponding edges and corners and join each side of that hexagon as you did the first one.

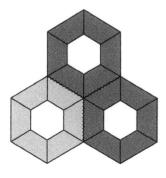

Continue adding hexagons to complete your floral design, frequently checking your project's fabric key and assembly diagram for the correct number and placement of fabric-covered patches.

DESIGNER ALERT
When making floral units, it's easier to add hexagons in a circular pattern, from the center out. When working on larger designs, entire sections of a design are completed and then sewn together. (See "Cattails and Butterflies" on page 43.)

Once you're finished adding hexagons, knot the thread end and bury a length of thread by traveling under the seam allowance a distance before trimming. Be sure you do not go through the paper template.

REMOVE THE SURROUNDED PAPER TEMPLATES

Pieced designs sometimes become unwieldy, stiff, or heavy because of all the templates inside the hexagons. If that happens, you can remove the template from any hexagon that is completely surrounded by other fabric-covered hexagons. It's easiest to remove templates at this stage, before the piece is appliquéd onto the background. However, template removal isn't absolutely necessary until an entire floral unit is complete, and designs with paper templates inside them hold their overall shape better, making them easier to appliqué to your background. You'll have to decide when it's best to remove your templates based on each individual project.

If you do decide to remove surrounded paper templates at this stage, the process is simple. Clip the desired hexagon's basting threads and gently pull the threads out. Hold the unit with the wrong side facing you, and use the nail on your index finger to gently press up from the right side of the hexagon. Generally the paper template will pop up and out. If it does not, carefully pull back a seam allowance and use tweezers to gently grab the template edge and pull it out.

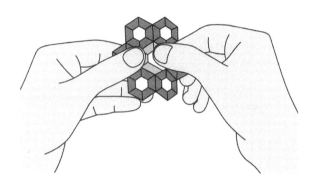

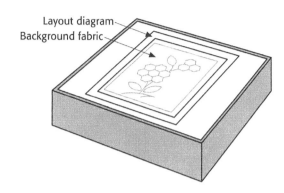

DESIGNER ALERT

Don't remove the paper templates from the outer edges of a floral design until the unit has been appliquéd onto the background fabric! *Early removal of the basting threads and paper templates from the outer design edges will cause the seam allowances to unfold and the design to lose its shape.*

PREPARE THE BACKGROUND FABRIC

You may need to prepare the background fabric before attaching the floral units to your quilt top. Refer to your project's directions; not all projects require all the steps listed below.

1. Find the floral arrangement layout diagram for your project and use a photocopier to enlarge it by the percentage specified. This will allow you to trace the pattern at full size. (Some of the patterns will have to be enlarged in several sections and then pieced together, because the finished size of the arrangement is larger than a standard-sized piece of copy paper.)

2. Place the layout diagram over a light table or another light source and position the background fabric on top of it, right side up.

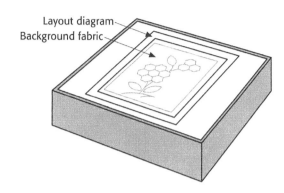

Layout diagram
Background fabric

3. Use a water-soluble marker or fine-line pencil to very lightly trace stem lines, flower and leaf positions, and container and accessory locations on the right side of the background fabric.

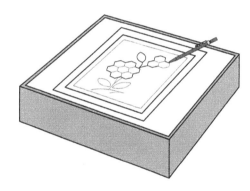

4. Remove the fabric from the light table. Embroider, fuse, or appliqué any stems, vines, and leaves that create the outline of the design or will be tucked under the hexagonal floral units. (See "Appliqué Techniques for Fabric Florists" on page 18 for detailed instructions on these techniques.)

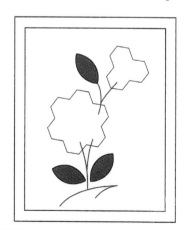

APPLIQUÉ THE FLORAL UNIT TO THE BACKGROUND

Once the floral units have been pieced together and the background fabric is prepared, it's time to permanently attach the floral units. Using the lightly traced floral locations as a guide, lay the pieced hexagonal units in place on the right side of the background fabric. Pin in place to hold. Use contrasting-colored thread to baste these units in place.

Use your desired hand or machine method to appliqué each floral unit in place with thread that matches the floral unit fabric. (See "Appliqué Stitches" on page 21.)

REMOVE THE PAPER TEMPLATES FROM THE OUTER-EDGE HEXAGONS

Once a floral unit has been appliquéd to the background fabric, the remaining paper templates must be removed. Remove any basting stitches from the front of the appliquéd floral unit. Turn the background fabric over, locate the floral unit, and—using the smallest scissors you have, such as appliqué or embroidery scissors—carefully slit the background fabric behind the floral unit. Insert the point of your scissors and cut

away the background fabric at least ¼" *inside* the appliqué stitching line. Leave more seam allowance if you wish; you can always trim it away later. Make sure you do not cut the fabric of your paper-pieced hexagons.

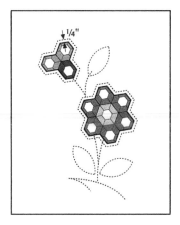

Remove the paper templates by using the nail of your index finger to pop each template out. If a template doesn't pop out easily, use tweezers to remove it. Make sure all paper templates have been removed before quilting; by that point, it's too late!

DESIGNER ALERT
If you take good care of your paper templates, you might get two or three uses out of them before you have to buy or make new ones. I store my reusable templates in snack-sized plastic zipper bags.

ADD BORDERS

Each project contains directions for cutting and attaching borders to your appliquéd quilt top. If you're designing your own quilt, you can determine what length to cut your border strips by measuring the quilt through the center vertically to add side borders or horizontally to add top and bottom borders.

Appliqué Techniques for Fabric Florists

The floral bouquets in this book use a few special appliqué techniques (bias stems, fusible appliqué, and basic appliqué) that may be new to you. Use these techniques, each of which is described in detail below, to add dimension, line, and detail to your floral arrangement.

MAKING ⅛" BIAS STEMS

Several of the floral arrangements in this book use ⅛" folded bias strips as stems. They contribute a heavier design line (one with height and width), texture, and weight to the arrangements. Cut bias strips from a selection of different green fabrics to add interest and variety to your floral design. Making these stems is quite easy.

1. Rotary cut bias strips ⅜" to ½" wide in a variety of lengths. (Consult your project directions to determine approximately how many inches of bias stems you'll need and in what lengths.) The finished stems don't have to be exactly ⅛" wide; use stems that are a bit wider for larger flowers and a bit skinnier for leaves and small flower buds. Fabric strips can be long (12" to 15") or short (2" to 3"), because they will be cut to a variety of lengths when finished.

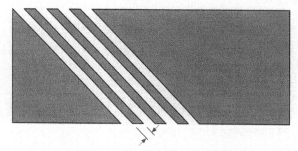

Cut ⅜"- to ½"-wide strips on the bias.

2. Lay out a length of bias strip on your ironing board, wrong side up. Spray the strip with sizing.

> **DESIGNER ALERT**
> *Place a piece of muslin over your ironing surface to protect it from repeatedly being sprayed with sizing. When the muslin becomes stiff or soiled from sizing buildup, simply throw it into the washer and dryer, and then reuse it.*

3. Set your iron to hot. Fold the top one-third of the strip down lengthwise, wrong sides together. Press, being careful to press only the folded part of the bias strip. (You don't want to dry out the bottom edge. If you try to respray the strip, the first folded edge will unfold, and you'll have to begin again.)

Fold down the top one-third of the strip and press.

4. Next, fold the bottom third of the bias strip up and over the first fold; press. Try to work quickly, because if the strip is still damp with the spray sizing, it will hold a sharp crease.

Fold up the bottom edge of the strip and press.

5. When it's time to use your bias stems, choose a stem that's ½" to 1" longer than you need for your design; the long ends will be tucked under other appliqué pieces, such as flowers or leaves. Use a running stitch to temporarily baste the stems in place, fold side down, on your background fabric. Then permanently appliqué down both sides, either by hand or machine. The raw edge ends, as well as your assembly mechanics, will be hidden when the stems are tucked under other pieces.

If your design calls for exposed stem ends, baste and appliqué as described above, but as you appliqué, fold or tuck under the exposed raw edges of the bias stem, just as you would an appliqué leaf point. Slightly angle the end of the stem as if it had been cut by a garden knife. (You'll use this technique in "Bow-Tied Bundle" on page 39.)

Fold under
at an angle.

FUSING FOR EASIER APPLIQUÉ

A fast and easy method for adding leaves, foliage, and message letters to your floral arrangements is to fuse them with commercially available fusible adhesive, a bonding agent that is ironed onto the wrong side of the appliqués and then ironed onto your quilt top. This method only provides a temporary bond, so each of the appliqué shapes must then be permanently sewn down, either by hand or machine.

There are many brands of fusible webbing on the market, so check the manufacturer's directions for specifics concerning the proper iron temperature setting and ironing time. Follow these steps to appliqué with fusible web.

1. Select a leaf or lettering pattern (either follow your project's directions or see pages 77–78 for possible options). Notice that your fusible web has two sides: one side has a smooth paper surface, and the other has a bumpy, fusible-adhesive surface. Trace your patterns onto the smooth paper side. Remember to *reverse any lettering or asymmetrical shapes when tracing* or they will be backward when you try to use them on your quilt. *Do not* include seam allowances when tracing your patterns.

Trace on the paper side of the fusible web.
Reverse any letters and asymmetrical shapes.

2. Following the manufacturer's directions, iron the fusible web onto the wrong side of your appliqué fabric. For small letters and leaves, fuse across the entire back of the shape. However, if the piece is large and you're concerned about stiffness, simply trim away the center section of the webbing inside your pattern, about ⅛" to ¼" from the outer edge, *before* fusing it to your appliqué fabric.

Center trimmed away

3. Cut out each appliqué shape on the traced line. Remember—don't add seam allowances.

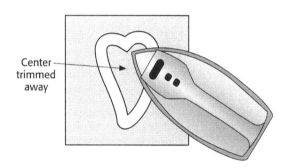

4. Peel off the paper backing, leaving the adhesive on the back of each appliqué shape.

5. Place each shape where desired on the right side of your background fabric, adhesive side down. (Now is the time to make sure nothing was incorrectly reversed during the tracing process.) When you're satisfied that your design is placed correctly, follow the manufacturer's directions to fuse.

DESIGNER ALERT
When fusing letters and foliage, use a press cloth to prevent any iron marks on the surface of the fabric. This is especially important when using Ultrasuede.

6. Permanently attach these appliqué pieces to the background fabric by stitching around the outer edges. Use a matching thread color or a decorative, contrasting thread color. There are several different ways you can do this:

- A running or straight stitch about ¹⁄₁₆" inside the edge of each piece.

- A blanket stitch around each piece, done either by machine or hand.

- A blind hem stitch, done by machine, with clear monofilament thread or colored thread.

- A machine satin stitch.

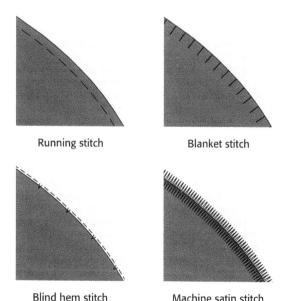

Running stitch

Blanket stitch

Blind hem stitch

Machine satin stitch

APPLIQUÉ STITCHES

Appliqué is the process of attaching one layer of fabric to the surface of another layer of fabric. It can be done by hand or machine. Experiment with both methods and use whichever method you prefer in your projects.

Hand Appliqué Stitch

Hand-appliqué stitches should be small, close together, and somewhat tight, as they hold the appliqué piece in place. The stitch should be almost invisible because it wraps around the edge of the appliqué shape and does not travel over the top of the appliqué piece. Use this method for English paper piecing or other appliqué pieces that have their raw edges turned under, but not for fused appliqués.

1. Set the prepared hexagonal floral unit in position, wrong side down on the background fabric.

2. Baste the floral unit in place with a running stitch. Be careful not to pull the threads too tightly.

3. Thread a needle with a single strand of thread that matches the unit color. Knot the end and trim off any long tail.

4. Insert the needle from the back of the background fabric, coming up just under a folded edge of the floral unit. Bring the needle out the side of the folded edge, catching only the edge of the fabric, not the paper template.

5. Reinsert the needle through the background fabric only, right next to the folded edge of the floral unit and right beside the stitch you brought up in step 4.

6. Travel a very short distance under the background fabric and come up again, just catching the edge of the appliqué piece, as in step 4. Repeat to completely attach the unit, tacking down the points of the hexagon as you go.

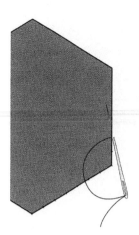

Machine Appliqué

If speed is a concern, try appliquéing your floral units by machine using a basic blind hem stitch. Machine appliqué works especially well with ½" hexagonal templates and may be used with fused pieces. Machine appliquéing makes it possible to complete an arrangement in less than half the time required to do the project by hand. When machine appliquéing, select a very short stitch length, and use a very narrow (almost 0) stitch width, which just barely catches the folded edge, *not* the enclosed paper template. Experiment on a practice piece of fabric to get the hang of the technique before you begin working on your project.

Floral Embellishments

Several different techniques and elements are used to add detail and texture to the projects in this book. Some of these, such as embroidered stems and vines, are completed before appliquéing the floral units to the background fabric. Others, such as beads, bells, or buttons, are added after quilting.

EMBROIDERY STITCHES

The projects in this book use several basic embroidery stitches to represent flower stems and tendrils and to outline words and letters. If you're unfamiliar with the stitches, take some time to practice them on scrap fabric before working directly on your project.

I generally use two strands of embroidery floss to work these stitches. If I want a heavier line, I'll use anywhere from three to six strands. Either a quilting or an appliqué needle will work for these embroidery stitches—just be sure that the needle you choose has a large enough eye to accommodate the number of strands of thread that you're using.

Blanket Stitch

This is an excellent *visible* stitch to use to attach leaves and letters, and it can be done by hand or machine. It finishes the edges of your fused units and provides a decorative, as well as functional, outline to your appliqué pieces. The hand-stitching method is described below. See your machine manual to determine how to create this look by machine.

1. Thread your needle with the desired number of strands of embroidery floss and knot the end.

2. Working from left to right, insert the needle from the back of the background fabric, coming up just at the outside edge of a leaf or letter, at point A.

3. Insert the needle at point B, slightly to the right of and above point A, going through the appliqué fabric as well as the background fabric.

4. Bring the needle back out of the fabric at point C, right at the edge of the appliqué leaf or letter. Before pulling the needle through, make sure the floss is under the point of the needle.

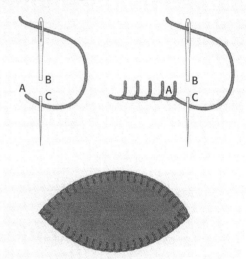

5. Gently pull the floss taut, but not too tight.

6. Continue along the edge of each leaf or letter, maintaining an even tension all the way around. Make sure that you keep the height of your stitches even throughout.

DESIGNER ALERT
Consider using a contrasting thread color for a decorative accent.

Chain Stitch

To create thicker embroidered stems and vines, use the basic chain stitch, described here. (See "Grandmother's Flower Garden" on page 52.)

1. Thread your needle with the desired number of strands of embroidery floss and knot the end.

2. Pull the needle and floss up and through the background fabric at point A.

3. Reinsert the needle back into the same hole at point A, and bring it out at point B, creating a loop of floss. Make sure the loop is *under* the needle and that the needle is going through the loop.

4. Gently pull the needle through the loop, creating a small teardrop shape. Don't pull too tightly.

5. Point B now becomes point A for the next stitch. Continue making stitches as described in steps 2 through 4 above, always inserting the needle into the hole made by the emerging floss.

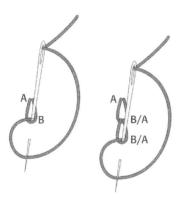

6. To end the line of stitches, take a small stitch over the last chain stitch to tack it down.

DESIGNER ALERT
When working on fabric floral arrangements, make the rows of chain stitches a bit longer than needed so the ends can be tucked under the appliquéd floral units.

Flat, Straight Stitch

This is the stitch you'll use to join the edges and corners of individual hexagonal fabric patches. The stitch closes the gap between the edges and assures that your pieces will lie flat on your background fabric.

1. Thread your needle with 100%-cotton sewing thread and knot the end.

2. Holding two adjoining hexagon edges *flat* next to one another, insert your needle under one folded seam allowance and bring it out at a corner at point A. Reinsert the needle at point B and bring it back out at point C, three or four fabric fibers from your first stitch. Pull the stitches taught to close the gap. Reinsert the needle at D, and repeat until you reach the corner, easing in any extra fabric as you go. Take a final stitch right in the corner.

3. Before adding another hexagon in the same manner, make sure that your corners are matched up. If they aren't matched up, pull out the stitches and restitch that side, easing in the fabric as you go. (These edges are primarily bias, so any excess fabric can be eased in easily.)

4. When you reach the end of a side, take an extra stitch or two, and knot the thread.

Running Stitch

This stitch is used to baste the fabric hexagons to their paper templates, and then later to baste the floral units to the background fabric before appliquéing. It can also be used to decoratively attach fused leaves and letters.

1. Thread a needle with a single strand of the thread of your choice.

2. Bring the needle up at point A, down at point B, then back up at point C. If you're using the running stitch for decorative stitches that will remain in your project, try to make your stitches the same length on the right and wrong sides, or uniformly longer on the right side.

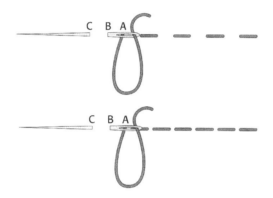

Stem Stitch

Also known as an outline stitch or backstitch, I use the stem stitch to add floral stems, vines, and tendrils to my arrangements. It produces a very narrow stitched row or outline, or it can be repeated in close parallel rows to create wider stems.

1. Thread your needle with the desired number of strands of embroidery floss and knot the end.

2. Working from left to right, bring the needle up from the fabric at point A. (If possible, you should begin where the knot will be hidden behind a floral unit, or else gently weave the thread tail into the back of your stitches as you work.)

3. Insert the needle at point B, and bring it up at point C, halfway between points A and B. Note that the needle must be moved a step backward before a step is taken forward along the stitch row.

4. Repeat to the end of the line, spacing the stitches evenly and always keeping your working thread below your needle, as shown.

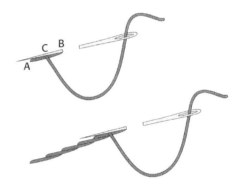

5. Bury the thread end by weaving it into the line of stitching on the wrong side of the fabric.

LETTERING

Several of the floral arrangements feature written messages. Carefully consider the method and materials to use for these messages. You want the letters to stand out, be easily read, and have sharp, clear edges. For "Welcome Home" (page 67), I used block letters cut from Ultrasuede and attached with fusible appliqué. Ultrasuede is a great choice for lettering because it adds depth and texture, the edges don't ravel, and the letters and points remain sharp and clear. For "Blessed Friendship" (page 35), I used inked and embroidered script, which looks handwritten and therefore adds a more personal touch to the piece.

Block Letters

These letters can be hand or machine appliquéd using your favorite appliqué method. I used the fusible technique, followed by machine straight stitching.

1. Follow the project directions to select the message and letters needed, being sure to check your

spelling carefully. If you're writing your own message, I've included a complete block-letter alphabet (see page 77).

2. Enlarge or reduce the letters to the appropriate size, if necessary, depending on the space allowed and message length.

3. Trace the letters *in reverse* on the paper side of the fusible webbing of your choice.

4. Refer to "Fusing for Easier Appliqué" (page 19), and follow steps 1 through 6.

Embroidered Script Lettering

For a more delicate look, you can ink or embroider the lettering on your quilts. For the "Blessed Friendship" quilt (page 35), I lettered *Friendship—Blessed are those who enjoy its warmth . . .* in a script format (see page 38). Such small lettering could not be appliquéd, so I simply traced it in place and embroidered over the tracing. (For a complete script alphabet, see page 78.)

1. Follow the project directions or write out your desired message in the appropriate size and style on a sheet of paper.

2. Place the message on a light table or another light source, message side up, and secure it with tape.

3. Place the pieced quilt top over the message, and position it so the message is in the correct spot. Secure the quilt top in place with tape.

4. Choose a permanent ink, fine-line marker in a color that matches the embroidery thread you'll use for your message. Using the marker, carefully and clearly trace the message onto the front of the quilt top.

5. Use a single strand of matching embroidery floss to sew a small stem stitch (see page 24) outlining the letters for greater dimension and texture. Pull the stitches taut.

BEADING

Beads can be added to create clusters of berries or sprigs of baby's breath. Look closely at "Bow-Tied Bundle" (page 39). The seed-bead berry clusters add to the realism of the arrangement; serve as filler material; and give the piece sparkle, color, and glitz.

DESIGNER ALERT
While beading is part of the quilt-embellishment process, remember that it is a step you should perform after *you have quilted, bound, and otherwise finished your quilt.*

To apply beads to your project:

1. Cut a length of thread and knot it, leaving only a short tail.

2. Starting from the back side of your quilt sandwich (backing, batting, and quilt top), go through all three layers. Pop the knot through the backing fabric and hide the thread tail between the layers.

3. Come up through the quilt top; then go back down through all three layers, only a fiber or two away from your initial hole.

4. Come back up through all three layers, almost on top of the first hole, to create a lock stitch.

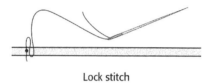

Lock stitch

5. String a bead onto your thread.

6. Go down through the fabric and come up again in the same spot where you began. Go through the bead a second time; this will make the bead stand up on its side, and will more securely attach it.

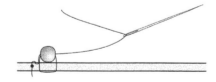

7. Add as many beads as your project requires, going through each bead twice.

8. When beading is complete, knot the thread, pop it between the layers of the project, and bury a length of thread.

Finishing Your Quilt

After the flower pattern has been assembled, the arrangement has been appliquéd to the background fabric, and the surrounding borders have been added, it's time to complete your quilt. In this section you'll find all you need to know to finish your fabric floral arrangements.

LAYERING AND BASTING

Before beginning to quilt, you need to anchor the layers of your quilt together. The careful basting you do now will mean easier quilting later.

1. Prewash the backing and batting, if needed. (Check the batting manufacturer's instructions.)

2. Cut the backing fabric and batting 4" to 6" larger than the pieced top, or refer to your project's materials list for the correct size.

3. Place the backing fabric right side down on a flat work surface and secure it in several places with masking tape. Spread the batting on top of the backing. Smooth it down and secure it with tape as well. Finally, center the pieced top, right side up, onto the batting and backing. Smooth it out from the center.

4. Beginning in the center and working out, baste the layers together. Baste with thread for hand quilting and baste with size 0 or 1 rustproof safety pins for machine quilting. Space basting stitches or pins 2" to 3" apart.

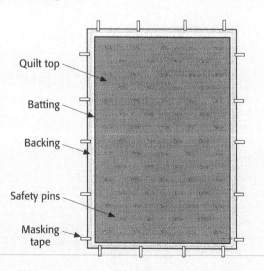

Quilt top

Batting

Backing

Safety pins

Masking tape

QUILTING

The main advantage of my technique for English paper piecing is that I've eliminated the background hexagons, creating large open areas in the background fabric and borders. These are perfect places to showcase great quilting designs.

When choosing quilting designs, keep the twofold purpose of quilting in mind:

- To add enough quilting to permanently bond the layers.
- To enhance the piecework and appliqué by bringing dimension and depth to the quilt top.

I use several different quilting techniques to meet these two objectives, and they're presented here in the order in which I usually add them to a quilt. Each one has been used in at least one of the projects in this book, and each quilting design can be used either individually or in combination with the others. I hope these designs will inspire you to start quilting—and to complete your floral designs. But remember that the quilting designs you select should depend, most importantly, on your own preferences and skill level.

DESIGNER ALERT
I machine quilted all of the quilts in this book on my home sewing machine, but the open areas and borders would also be great places to show off your hand-quilting skills.

In-the-Ditch Quilting

Start by sewing in the ditch (on the seams) of the borders. This anchors the quilt top in place, preventing any shifting as you add more involved quilting. In addition, quilt in the ditch around the outside edges of stems, tendrils, leaves, baskets, and flowers. Such stitching causes the curves, angles, and edges of each appliqué or embroidered element to stand out more clearly and precisely. Next, within each arrangement, identify individual floral units, and carefully quilt in the seam lines around those units. For instance, "Wreath for All Seasons" (page 71) contains many different floral types within the wreath itself: six-petaled posies, radiating blooms, single buds, and berry clusters, as well as a large bow. Each of these was outlined with in-the-ditch quilting, making each flower type a separate, complete unit.

Outline Quilting

After quilting in the ditch around the floral designs, you can add additional lines of stitching ⅛" to ¼" from the in-the-ditch stitching. This tends to flatten the immediate area around each floral unit and around the overall floral arrangement, making the design really "pop."

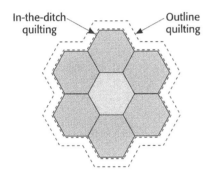

In addition, I sometimes use outline quilting *inside* floral units, about ⅛" inside the seam lines. This better defines each floral unit, making each one appear even more distinct from the surrounding hexagons or background fabric.

Free-Floating Quilt Designs

If you're looking for quilting inspiration, you can look to the theme of your project; try quilting patterns or shapes that reflect or repeat the pieced floral designs. The background of "Wreath for All Seasons" (page 71) has a holly berry and leaf design quilted in each

background corner and in each outer-border corner square, echoing the Christmas theme.

The remaining background of "Wreath for All Seasons" has a quilted grid of randomly spaced wavy lines.

Feather Quilting

The floral designs in this book provide excellent areas for feather quilting, both on the background fabric and within borders. Some feather designs are fairly simple and straightforward (see "A Spring Basket from Grandmother's Garden" on page 32), while others are much more intricate and detailed (see "Bow-Tied Bundle" on page 39 and "Sunflower Bouquet" on page 58).

Quilted Grids

A very fast and easy way to fill in large background areas is to use a grid of diamonds or squares. The straight, parallel lines complement the curves in the floral arrangements. (See "Blessed Friendship" on page 35 and "Sunflower Bouquet" on page 58.)

Stipple Quilting

Many of the background areas of my quilts are quilted with an allover stipple stitch, which gives the background a bubbly texture that is very appealing both visually and tactilely. It also tends to flatten the background, allowing both the floral piecework and any free-floating quilt designs to come forward. For this reason, stipple quilting should be done last, after all other quilting is complete.

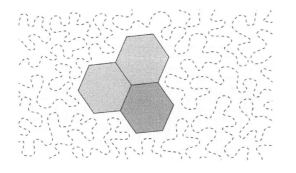

Fabric-Print Quilt Designs

One good option is to let your fabric make your quilting decisions for you. If a border fabric has a pleasing design, carefully stitch around the shapes printed on the fabric. One advantage to this approach is that it lets you get right to quilting because no marking is required.

Parallel Lines

Intricate quilting often gets lost in the design of border fabrics, so you may decide that it doesn't make sense to put a lot of time and creativity into quilting that will just go unnoticed. In these cases, I suggest quilting simple, straight, parallel lines, either running parallel to the quilt edges, as a frame, or perpendicular to the quilt edges. Both work well. (See "Topiary Rose" on page 63.)

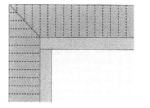 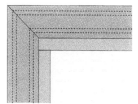

For a simple twist on the parallel lines theme, group double or even triple lines spaced at intervals.

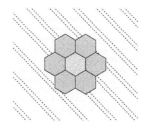 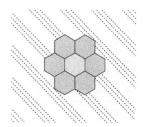

Simple Geometric Designs

I quilted many of the projects in this book with easily sewn geometric designs. Some appear within individual hexagonal patches (circles and smaller hexagon outlines sewn ⅛" inside the seam lines), while others were quilted on the background fabric and along border strips. The designs I quilted include wavy lines (single, facing, parallel, and free-form), loops (tall, short, or a combination of the two), and intersecting circles. Experiment with other designs that complement your design and fabric choices.

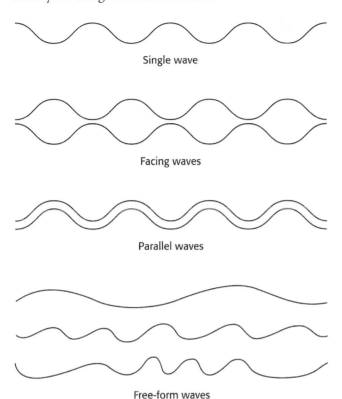

Single wave

Facing waves

Parallel waves

Free-form waves

Loops

Intersecting circles

ATTACHING A ROD POCKET

These fabric arrangements are usually displayed on a wall, so you'll need a sleeve of some type for inserting a hanging rod or dowel. Follow these steps to make a rod pocket.

1. Measure the width of your quilt at the top and subtract 2". Cut a fabric strip to that length and 5" to 9" wide, depending on the size of the rod you plan to use for hanging.

2. Press ¼" of fabric under at each end of the strip. Press each end under once again, and stitch ⅛" from the inside folded edge.

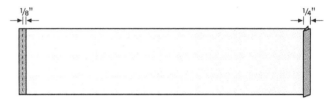

3. Fold the strip in half along its length, wrong sides together. Pin it together at the ends and at several points in between. Press.

4. Center the rod pocket on the back of the quilt at the upper edge, aligning the raw edges of the quilt and pocket. Pin the rod pocket in place. As you sew the binding to the upper edge of the quilt, you will automatically attach the rod pocket.

5. After you apply the binding, hemstitch the bottom edge of the rod pocket to the quilt back by hand. Be sure to sew through only the backing and batting, not the quilt top, and leave the ends of the sleeve open, sewing only the bottom edge of the rod pocket to the quilt.

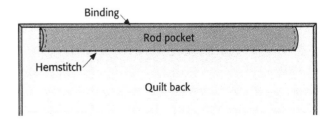

Binding

Rod pocket

Hemstitch

Quilt back

BINDING

After the quilt is quilted, it's time to bind the outer edges. Follow the steps below and your binding will be very neat, full of batting, and will have hidden binding ends.

1. Square up the quilt layers by trimming the excess batting and backing even with the top.

2. If you're making a project from this book, the project's cutting section will tell you how many and what size binding strips to cut. If you're making a project of your own design, use your rotary-cutting equipment to cut enough 2"-wide strips to go around the quilt, plus 6" to 8" for corners and finishing. Use diagonal seams to join the strips into one long binding strip. Press the seams open to reduce bulk.

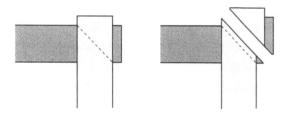

3. Press the binding in half along its length, wrong sides together and raw edges aligned.

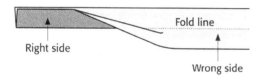

4. Beginning on one side, place the binding on the quilt top, aligning the raw edges of the binding with the raw edge of the quilt. Using a ¼" seam allowance and leaving an 8" tail at the beginning, stitch the binding to the quilt top, backstitching at the beginning and stopping ¼" from the corner; backstitch and remove the quilt from the machine.

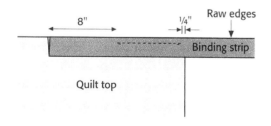

5. With the corner directly in front of you, fold the binding straight up, creating a 45° angle. Then fold the binding straight down, keeping the fold even with the edges of the quilt. The raw edges of the binding should now be even with the adjacent side of the quilt.

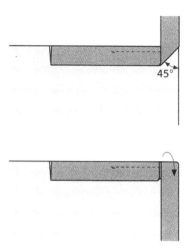

6. Begin stitching before the fabric at the corner. The new seam will be perpendicular to the previous one. Continue until you're ¼" from the next corner, and repeat step 5. Repeat for all four corners of the quilt, stopping 5" to 8" from where you originally began stitching. Backstitch.

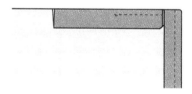

7. Remove the quilt from the machine and trim the binding, leaving an 8" tail. Lay the quilt flat on the ironing board and carefully fold the two tails together at the center. Press, creating easily seen creases on each strip.

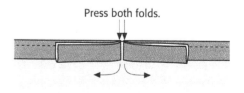

Press both folds.

8. Unfold the strip ends. Lay one strip flat, right side up. Lay the other right side down on top of it, matching the crease points on the edges. Carefully draw a diagonal line through the point where the fold lines meet. Stitch through the marked line.

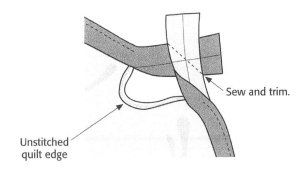

Sew and trim.

Unstitched quilt edge

9. Check to make sure the newly attached binding is the correct length. If the binding is correct, trim the tails ¼" from the seam. Finger-press the seam allowance open, refold the binding, and finish sewing the binding.

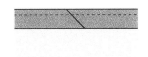

10. Gently fold the binding from the front of the quilt to the back and pin it in place. The binding should easily fold over the seam allowance and just cover the stitching line. Using thread that matches the binding, whipstitch the folded edge of the binding to the back of the quilt, being careful that your stitches don't go through to the front of the quilt. As you reach the corners, gently pull the binding straight out. With your thumbnail in the corner, fold over the unstitched binding edge, creating a mitered corner. Secure it with stitching. Repeat for all the corners of the quilt.

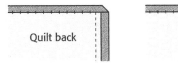

Quilt back

LABELING YOUR FABRIC FLORAL ARRANGEMENTS

Labeling your quilted floral arrangements is really an important finishing touch because it defines your quilts historically. How will future generations know who made this fabric floral design, or the details about it, if you don't sign it?

I make my labels on a piece of muslin, and I either print them by hand with permanent ink, or by computer using printer-safe fabric. I add a border before I appliqué the label to the back of the quilt, and I include some or all of the following information:

- Quilter's name
- Quilter's address
- Quilter's phone number
- Quilt title
- Quilt dimensions
- Date completed
- Techniques used
- Other special information about the fabrics or embellishments used, why the quilt was made, for whom it was made, and so on.

Let your label tell the story of your floral arrangement. Let it document your work, and give future owners the opportunity to share your "walk through Grandmother's garden."

A Spring Basket from Grandmother's Garden

This is the perfect floral arrangement for a beginner who is learning English paper piecing, or for anyone who has never worked with ¼" hexagons before. The basket and corner squares are full of brightly colored posies. There's room for some feather quilting in the center, and the whole arrangement is topped off with a silk ribbon bow and a dragonfly button. This is a great little floral arrangement for giving and sharing.

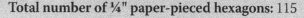
MATERIALS

Yardage is based on 42"-wide fabric.

¼ yard of green print for inner border and binding

⅛ yard of a small-scale, multicolored floral print for outer border

10" x 22" piece of light green tone-on-tone for background and outer-border corner squares

4" x 9" piece *each* of 2 different browns (medium and dark) for basket hexagons

4" x 9" piece *each* of 2 different greens for leaf hexagons

4" x 9" piece of yellow for flower hexagons

3" x 5" piece *each* of 2 different reds (medium and dark) for flower-center hexagons

3" x 9" piece of light pink for flower hexagons

2" x 9" piece of dark pink for flower hexagons

20" x 42" piece for backing and rod pocket

20" x 22" piece of batting

15" of 4-mm yellow silk ribbon for bow

Small butterfly, bug, or dragonfly button or charm

CUTTING

Cut the pieces listed below *before* cutting fabric for the hexagons.

From the light green tone-on-tone, cut:

- 1 rectangle, 10" x 12"
- 4 squares, 3" x 3"

From the green print, cut:

- 1 strip, 1½" x 42"; crosscut to make:
    2 strips, 1½" x 7½"
    2 strips, 1½" x 10½"
- 2 strips, 2" x 42"

From the multicolored floral print, cut:

- 1 strip, 3" x 42"; crosscut to make:
    2 strips, 3" x 9½"
    2 strips, 3" x 10½"

ASSEMBLE THE QUILT TOP

1. Refer to "English Paper Piecing Miniature Hexagons" (page 12) to prepare ¼" hexagons in the colors and quantities shown in the fabric key below. Use the basted hexagons to create the flower units below in the quantities specified.

Fabric key

- Dark brown (15)
- Medium brown (15)
- Yellow (18)
- Light pink (12)
- Dark pink (6)
- Greens (43)
- Medium red (3)
- Dark red (3)

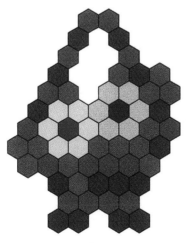

Make 1.

Make 1.

Make 1.

Make 2.

2. Baste the floral basket in the center of the 10" x 12" light green fabric rectangle. Appliqué the basket in place using matching thread. (See "Appliqué Stitches" on page 21.) Remove the basting stitches and paper templates.

3. Square up the background fabric to a 7½" x 8½" rectangle, being careful to center the spring basket.

4. Stitch the 1½" x 7½" green print strips to the top and bottom edges of the background rectangle. Press the seam allowances toward the green strips. Stitch the 1½" x 10½" green print strips to the sides of the rectangle. Press the seam allowances toward the green strips.

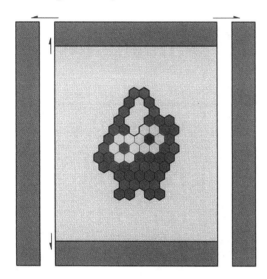

5. Sew the 3" x 9½" multicolored floral strips to the top and bottom edges of the quilt top. Press the seam allowances toward the floral strips. Stitch 3" x 3" light green squares to each end of both 3" x 10½" floral strips. Press the seam allowances away from the corner squares. Sew the pieced borders to the sides of the quilt. Press the seam allowances toward the floral strips.

6. Refer to the photo (page 32) to baste and appliqué the four floral units in place in the corner squares. Remove the basting stitches and paper templates.

COMPLETE THE ARRANGEMENT

Refer to "Finishing Your Quilt" (page 26).

1. Layer the quilt top with the batting and backing; baste.

2. Quilt as desired.

3. Square up the quilt top.

4. Add a rod pocket and bind the quilt using the 2" x 42" green print strips.

5. Make a silk ribbon bow and attach it to the top of the basket handle. Tack down the ends and loops, if desired. Attach a dragonfly button or charm, or other embellishments of your choice.

6. Label the back of your quilt.

Blessed Friendship

Stroll through Grandmother's garden, pick a few pretty blossoms, and send them to a special person with a message that says how much her friendship means to you. This quilt is similar to "Welcome Home" (page 67), except it uses ¼" hexagons, smaller borders, and script letters for the message, giving it a more personal look.

FINISHED QUILT: 13¼" x 14¾"
Total number of ¼" paper-pieced hexagons: 49

MATERIALS

Yardage is based on 42"-wide fabric.

⅓ yard of floral print for outer border and binding

⅛ yard of medium pink for middle border and flower hexagons

⅛ yard or scraps of dark green print for inner border

14" x 16" piece of cream print for background

4" x 9" piece *each* of purple and dark pink for flower hexagons

4" x 6" piece or scraps of dark green for appliquéd leaves

3" x 9" piece of medium green for flower-base hexagons

3" x 3" piece of periwinkle for flower hexagons

½ yard for backing and rod pocket

18" x 20" piece of batting

Embroidery thread in dark green, medium green, and black for stems, tendrils, and message lettering

Butterfly charm or button (optional)

Permanent fabric marker for lettering (I suggest a Pigma pen.)

CUTTING

Cut the pieces listed below *before* cutting fabric for the hexagons.

From the dark green for the inner border, cut:

- 1 strip, ⅝" x 42"; crosscut to make:
    2 strips, ⅝" x 8"
    2 strips, ⅝" x 9¾"

From the medium pink, cut:

- 1 strip, 1" x 42"; crosscut to make:
    2 strips, 1" x 8¼"
    2 strips, 1" x 10¾"

From the floral print, cut:

- 2 strips, 2½" x 42"; crosscut to make:
    2 strips, 2½" x 9¼"
    2 strips, 2½" x 14¾"
- 2 strips, 2" x 42"

ASSEMBLE THE QUILT TOP

1. Refer to "English Paper Piecing Miniature Hexagons" (page 12) to prepare ¼" hexagons in the colors and quantities shown in the fabric key below. Use the basted hexagons to create the flower units below in the quantities specified.

Fabric key

- Dark pink (12)
- Purple (13)
- Medium pink (13)
- Periwinkle (3)
- Medium green (8)

Make 1.   Make 1.   Make 1.   Make 1.   Make 1.   Make 1.

Make 1.   Make 1.   Make 1.   Make 2.

2. Use the template at the bottom of the page to make and prepare 12 leaves for appliqué or fusing. (See "Fusing for Easier Appliqué" on page 19.)

DESIGNER ALERT

I made my leaves from Ultrasuede and fused them; then I machine straight stitched ¹⁄₁₆" inside the leaf edges to permanently attach them to the background fabric.

3. Enlarge the floral arrangement layout diagram (page 38) by 110% and use it as a pattern to lightly trace the stem lines, tendrils, leaf, and flower locations onto the 14" x 16" cream print background fabric.

4. Using the stem stitch and two strands of embroidery thread, embroider the flower stems (dark green) and tendrils (medium green) over your tracings. (See "Stem Stitch" on page 24.)

5. Baste the prepared floral units in place on the background fabric. Appliqué the units in place using matching thread. Remove the basting stitches and paper templates.

6. Square up the background fabric to 8" x 9½", trimming so the floral arrangement is in the lower-right corner.

7. Sew the ⅝" x 8" dark green strips to the top and bottom of the background rectangle. Press the seam allowances toward the green strips. Sew the ⅝" x 9¾" dark green strips to the sides of the rectangle. Press the seam allowances toward the green strips.

8. Sew the 1" x 8¼" pink strips to the top and bottom edges of the quilt top. Press the seam allowances toward the pink strips. Sew the 1" x 10¾" pink strips to the sides of the quilt top. Press the seam allowances toward the pink strips.

9. Sew the 2½" x 9¼" floral strips to the top and bottom edges of the quilt top. Press the seam allowances toward the floral strips. Sew the 2½" x 14¾" floral strips to the sides of the quilt top. Press the seam allowances toward the floral strips.

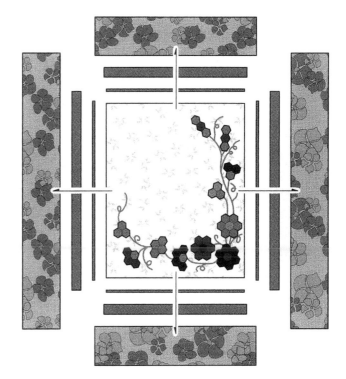

10. Using the message on page 38 (or one of your own created with the letters on page 78), trace and embroider the letters in the open space toward the upper left of the background area. (See "Embroidered Script Lettering" on page 25.)

11. Place the leaves as indicated, or where they're needed as filler, and baste or fuse them in place; then permanently appliqué the leaves in place.

COMPLETE THE ARRANGEMENT

Refer to "Finishing Your Quilt" (page 26).

1. Layer the quilt top with the batting and backing; baste.

2. Quilt as desired.

3. Square up the quilt top.

4. Add a rod pocket and bind the quilt using the 2" x 42" floral strips.

5. Attach the butterfly charm or button, or other embellishments of your choice.

6. Label the back of your quilt.

Leaf
Cut 12.

Pattern does not include seam allowance.

Fabric key

- Dark pink
- Purple
- Medium pink
- Periwinkle
- Medium green
- Dark green

Embroidery placement

*Friendship —
Blessed are those
who enjoy
its warmth...*

Floral arrangement layout diagram
Enlarge 110%.

Bow-Tied Bundle

Sometimes the tiniest embellishments can add just the right amount of sparkle
to a quilt. This is the case with these seed-bead berry clusters. They're subtly
mixed in with bunches of blooms, and the entire bouquet is tied up with
a bow. Anyone would be delighted to receive this floral bundle.

MATERIALS

Yardage is based on 42"-wide fabric.

¾ yard of dark green print for bias stems, leaf
hexagons, outer border, and binding

⅛ yard or scrap of dark pink for inner border and bow,
flower centers, and appliquéd border

14" x 22" piece of white for background

9" x 11" piece of light green floral print for flower
hexagons*

⅔ yard for backing and rod pocket

24" x 30" piece of batting

Embroidery thread in dark green for berry-cluster
stems

110–125 pink seed beads for berries

*I fussy cut the flower hexagons, centering a small
printed flower in each one. If you're going to do this,
the yardage required may vary based on how far apart
the flowers are.*

CUTTING

Cut the pieces listed below *before* cutting fabric
for the hexagons.

From the dark pink, cut:

- 2 strips, ¾" x 42"; crosscut to make:

    2 strips, ¾" x 10½"

    2 strips, ¾" x 18"

From the dark green print, cut:

- 2 strips, 3" x 42"; crosscut to make:

    2 strips, 3" x 11"

    2 strips, 3" x 23"

- 3 strips, 2" x 42"

ASSEMBLE THE QUILT TOP

1. Refer to "English Paper Piecing Miniature Hexagons" (page 12) to prepare ¼" hexagons in the
   colors and quantities shown in the fabric key
   below. Use the basted hexagons to create the
   flower and border units in the quantities specified.

2. Make approximately 50" of bias stem, referring to
   "Making ⅛" Bias Stems" (page 18).

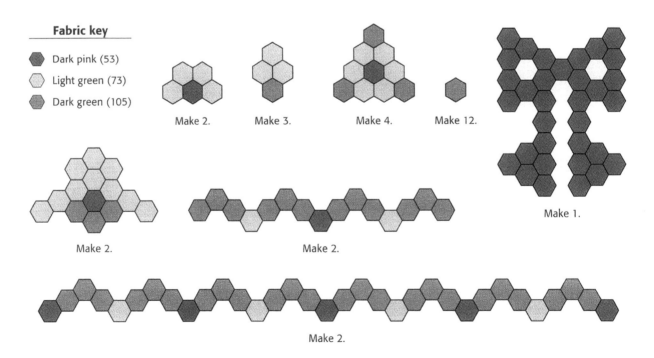

Fabric key

⬢ Dark pink (53)

⬡ Light green (73)

⬢ Dark green (105)

Make 2.

Make 3.

Make 4.

Make 12.

Make 1.

Make 2.

Make 2.

Make 2.

3. Enlarge the floral arrangement layout diagram on page 42 by 200% and use it as a pattern to lightly trace the stem lines, bow, and flower locations onto the 14" x 22" white background fabric. (Do not trace the stems for the seed-bead berry clusters yet.)

4. Baste the arrangement in place in the following order: bias stems, bow, flowers, and leaves. Appliqué the shapes into place using matching thread. Remove the basting stitches and paper templates.

5. Refer to the floral arrangement layout diagram (page 42) to lightly draw the stem lines for the seed-bead berry clusters. Embroider over these lines using a stem stitch and two strands of embroidery thread. (See "Stem Stitch" on page 24.)

6. Square up the background fabric to a 10½" x 17½" rectangle, being careful to center the floral arrangement.

7. Sew the ¾" x 10½" dark pink strips to the top and bottom edges of the background rectangle. Press the seam allowances toward the pink strips. Sew the ¾" x 18" pink strips to the sides of the rectangle. Press the seam allowances toward the pink strips.

8. Sew the 3" x 11" dark green print strips to the top and bottom of the quilt top. Press the seam allowances toward the dark green strips. Sew the 3" x 23" dark green strips to the sides of the quilt top. Press the seam allowances toward the dark green strips.

9. Refer to the floral arrangement layout diagram to carefully position the remaining floral units in each corner. Baste them in place. Place the hexagon borders along the edges of the background, making sure the end hexagons face the right directions. Baste them in place. Appliqué all the hexagon units permanently in place using matching thread.

COMPLETE THE ARRANGEMENT

Refer to "Finishing Your Quilt" (page 26).

1. Layer the quilt top with the batting and backing; baste.

2. Quilt as desired.

3. Square up the quilt top.

4. Add a rod pocket and bind the quilt using the 2" x 42" dark green strips.

5. Add the seed bead embellishments to the embroidered stems. (See "Beading" on page 25.)

6. Label the back of your quilt.

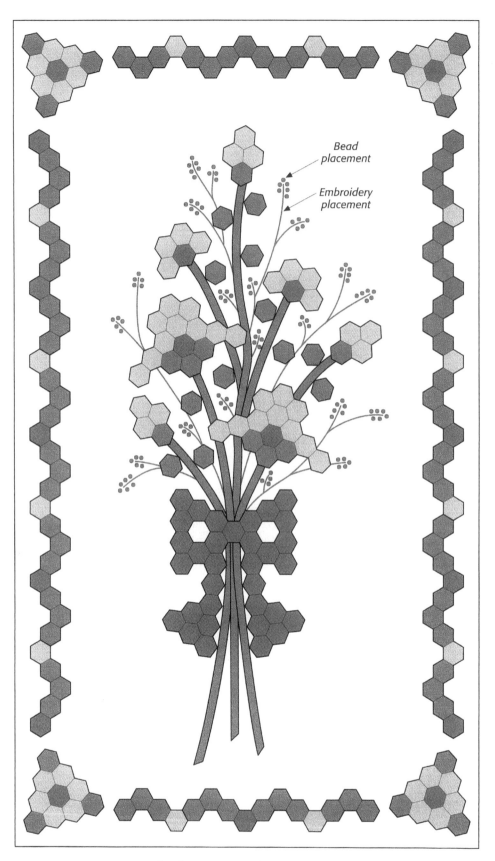

Fabric key

- Dark pink
- Light green
- Dark green

Bead placement

Embroidery placement

Floral arrangement layout diagram
Enlarge 200%.

Cattails and Butterflies

Although it's small, this little landscape speaks volumes in terms of serenity, peace, and solitude. Feel the gentle breeze ripple the water and watch the butterflies flutter from one cattail to another as the marsh marigolds turn their faces to the sun. Breathe deeply and enjoy this tiny bit of landscape beauty.

MATERIALS

Yardage is based on 42"-wide fabric.

¼ yard of dark green tone-on-tone print for outer border and binding

⅛ yard of medium green print for inner border

⅛ yard or scraps of medium gold for middle border and marsh-marigold hexagons

4" x 9" piece *each* of 4 to 6 assorted blue fabrics for sky hexagons

12" x 15" piece of light pastel print for background

6" x 9" piece of medium brown print for outer-border corner squares and cattail hexagons

5" x 9" piece of dark green print for bush hexagons

5" x 9" piece of medium blue for water hexagons

4" x 9" piece of medium green #1 for bush hexagons

4" x 9" piece of medium green #2 for marsh-grass hexagons

4" x 9" piece of green-and-cream print for marsh-reed hexagons

4" x 9" piece of light blue for water hexagons

3" x 9" piece of dark blue for water hexagons

3" x 9" piece of light green for bush hexagons

2" x 5" piece or scrap of red print for butterfly hexagons

20" x 42" piece for backing and rod pocket

20" x 22" piece of batting

Embroidery thread in light green, medium green, dark green, black, brown, and dark blue for cattail stems and leaves, butterfly bodies and antennae, cattail tops, and water ripples

DESIGNER ALERT
When piecing the sky of this quilt, I arranged my fabrics to form light clouds and give the appearance of a dark horizon. Play with the arrangement of your various blues before stitching them together.

CUTTING

Cut the pieces listed below *before* cutting fabric for the hexagons.

From the medium green print, cut:

● 2 strips, 1¼" x 42"; crosscut to make:
  2 strips, 1¼" x 10"
  2 strips, 1¼" x 13"

From the medium gold, cut:

● 2 strips, ¾" x 42"; crosscut to make:
  2 strips, ¾" x 11½"
  2 strips, ¾" x 13½"

From the dark green tone-on-tone print, cut:

● 2 strips, 1¾" x 42"; crosscut to make:
  2 strips, 1¾" x 12"
  2 strips, 1¾" x 13½"
● 2 strips, 2" x 42"

From the medium brown print, cut:

● 4 squares, 1¾" x 1¾"

ASSEMBLE THE QUILT TOP

This quilt is more like a traditional Grandmother's Flower Garden quilt than the others in this book; all the fabric-covered patches are sewn together in rows and sections rather than assembled as individual units.

1. Refer to "English Paper Piecing Miniature Hexagons" (page 12) to prepare ¼" hexagons in the colors and quantities shown in the fabric key on the facing page. Use the hexagons to construct the four sections shown. Remove the basting stitches and paper templates from all surrounded hexagons, leaving only those on the outer perimeter of the landscape.

Fabric key

- ⬢ Red print (4)
- ⬢ Medium brown (16)
- ⬢ Dark green (30)
- ⬢ Dark blue (12)
- ⬢ Medium green #2 (20)
- ⬢ Light green (10)
- ⬡ Light blue (22)
- ⬢ Medium green #1 (19)
- ⬡ Medium gold (16)
- ⬢ Medium blue (28)
- ⬢ Green and cream (21)
- ⬡ Assorted blues (100)

Section 1   Section 2   Section 3   Section 4

Layout diagram

2. Join the four landscape sections together using the same flat, straight stitch that you use to join individual hexagons to one another.

3. Baste your landscape onto the center of the 12" x 15" light pastel print background fabric; then appliqué it in place. Remove the remaining basting stitches and paper templates. Press.

4. Square up the background fabric to 10" x 11½", being careful to center the landscape.

5. Sew the 1¼" x 10" medium green strips to the top and bottom of the background rectangle. Press the seam allowances toward the green strips. Sew the 1¼" x 13" medium green strips to the sides of the rectangle. Press the seam allowances toward the green strips.

6. Sew the ¾" x 11½" medium gold strips to the top and bottom of the quilt top. Press the seam allowances toward the gold strips. Sew the ¾" x 13½" gold strips to the sides of the quilt top. Press the seam allowances toward the gold strips.

7. Sew the 1¾" x 12" dark green strips to the top and bottom of the quilt. Press the seam allowances

toward the green strips. Sew a 1¾" brown corner square to each end of both 1¾" x 13½" dark green strips. Press the seam allowances away from the corner squares. Sew the pieced strips to the sides of the quilt top. Press the seam allowances toward the dark green strips.

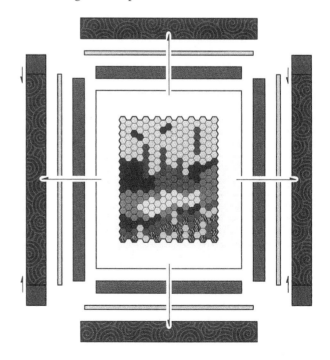

8. Refer to the placement lines below to lightly draw the stems, leaves, butterfly bodies and antennae, and water ripples onto your quilt. Embroider over the lines.

- Use six strands of light, medium, or dark green thread and a double line of stem stitches for the cattail stems. Refer to the photo on page 43 for color placement.

- Use six strands of light, medium, or dark green thread and a single line of stem stitches for the cattail leaves. (For each plant, use the shade of green that matches its stem.)

- Use two strands of thread and a single line of stem stitches for the butterfly bodies and antennae (black), the cattail tops (brown), and the ripples in the water (dark blue).

COMPLETE THE ARRANGEMENT

Refer to "Finishing Your Quilt" (page 26).

1. Layer the quilt top with the batting and backing; baste.

2. Quilt as desired.

3. Square up the quilt top.

4. Add a rod pocket and bind the quilt using the 2" x 42" dark green strips.

5. Label the back of your quilt.

Embroidery placement

Friendship Basket of Buttons and Blooms

Round buttons complement the hexagon flowers in this charming little quilt.
I quilted interlocking circles in the background to subtly echo the shape of
the buttons while adding texture and dimension to a wonderful arrangement.

MATERIALS

Yardage is based on 42"-wide fabric.

⅓ yard of floral print for outer border and binding

⅓ yard of blue for wide inner border and background

⅛ yard of brown print #1 for narrow inner borders and basket and border hexagons

9" x 22" piece of green print for bias stems and leaf and border hexagons

8" x 9" piece of red for flowers, flower center, and border hexagons

6" x 9" piece of yellow for flowers and border hexagons

2" x 9" piece of brown print #2 for basket hexagons

2" x 9" piece or scraps of pink for flower centers

⅔ yard for backing and rod pocket

22" x 25" piece of batting

Green embroidery thread for stems

24 blue buttons, ¼" diameter

Small snail button

CUTTING

Cut the pieces listed below *before* cutting fabric for the hexagons.

From the brown print #1, cut:

◎ 3 strips, ¾" x 42"; crosscut to make:

    2 strips, ¾" x 9¼"

    2 strips, ¾" x 10¾"

    2 strips, ¾" x 13¼"

    2 strips, ¾" x 14¾"

From the blue, cut:

◎ 1 rectangle, 12" x 14"

◎ 2 strips, 2¼" x 42"; crosscut to make:

    2 strips, 2¼" x 14"

    2 strips, 2¼" x 16"

From the floral print, cut:

◎ 3 strips, 2½" x 42"; crosscut to make:

    2 strips, 2½" x 19"

    2 strips, 2½" x 21"

◎ 2 strips, 2" x 42"

ASSEMBLE THE QUILT TOP

1. Refer to "English Paper Piecing Miniature Hexagons" (page 12) to prepare ¼" hexagons in the colors and quantities shown in the fabric key on the facing page. Use the basted hexagons to create the flower units, partial basket, and hexagon appliqué borders.

2. Make 15" to 20" of green print bias stems in a variety of lengths. (Refer to "Making ⅛" Bias Stems" on page 18.)

3. Use the floral arrangement layout diagram as a pattern to lightly trace the stem lines, basket placement, flower locations, and button tendrils onto the 12" x 14" blue background rectangle.

4. Baste the arrangement parts in place on the background, starting with the bias stems, then adding the basket unit, and finally placing the loose flowers and buds. Be sure all the raw edges of the bias stems are tucked under finished appliqué pieces. Appliqué the arrangement in place using matching thread. Remove the basting stitches and paper templates.

5. Embroider the button tendrils using two strands of embroidery thread and the stem stitch. (See "Stem Stitch" on page 24.)

6. Square up the background fabric to 8¾" x 10¾", being careful to center the floral arrangement.

7. Sew the ¾" x 10¾" brown print #1 strips to the sides of the quilt. Press toward the brown strips. Sew the ¾" x 9¼" brown print #1 strips to the top and bottom of the quilt. Press toward the brown strips.

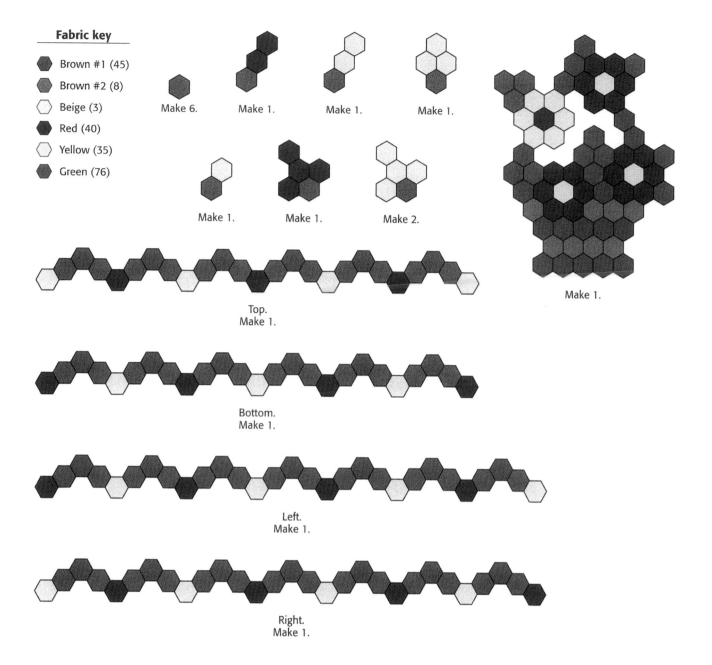

Fabric key

- Brown #1 (45)
- Brown #2 (8)
- Beige (3)
- Red (40)
- Yellow (35)
- Green (76)

Make 6.

Make 1.

Make 1.

Make 1.

Make 1.

Make 1.

Make 2.

Make 1.

Top.
Make 1.

Bottom.
Make 1.

Left.
Make 1.

Right.
Make 1.

8. Mark the center point of each edge of your quilt top. Mark the center points of the 2¼" x 14" blue strips and pin them to the quilt top and bottom, matching the center points. Starting and stopping ¼" from the edges of the quilt, sew the top and bottom blue borders to the quilt. Then mark the center points of the 2¼" x 16" blue strips and pin them to the sides of the quilt, matching the center points. Starting and stopping ¼" from the edges of the quilt, sew the side blue borders to the quilt.

9. Place the quilt top right side up on your ironing board. At one corner, let one strip lie flat while carefully folding the adjoining strip under at a 45° angle. (Use a square ruler with a 45° line to be sure your miter is at the correct angle and your corner is square.) Pin along this fold and press, creating an easily seen crease line.

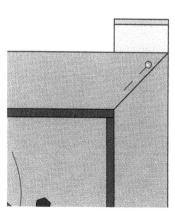

10. Unpin the fabrics and fold the quilt diagonally with right sides together so the crease can be seen on the back of the border. Repin and sew along the crease.

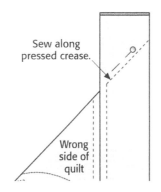

Sew along pressed crease.

Wrong side of quilt

11. Open the quilt top and make sure the seam is flat before trimming the seam allowances to ¼". Press the seam open. Repeat for the remaining corners.

12. Sew the ¾" x 14¾" brown print #1 strips to the sides of the quilt top. Press toward the brown strips. Sew the ¾" x 13¼" brown print #1 strips to the top and bottom of the quilt top. Press toward the brown strips.

13. Mark the center point of each edge of your quilt top again. Mark the center points of the 2½" x 19" floral strips and pin them to the quilt top and bottom, matching center points. Starting and stopping ¼" from the edges of the quilt, sew the top and bottom floral borders to the quilt. Then mark the center points of the 2½" x 21" floral strips and pin them to the quilt sides, matching center points. Starting and stopping ¼" from the edges of the quilt, sew the side floral borders to the quilt.

14. Repeat steps 9 through 11 to miter the outer floral border.

15. Carefully center the hexagon appliqué borders from step 1 (page 48) in the center of each blue border, noting the placement of the end hexagons. Baste the units in place and appliqué them to the quilt.

16. Use the tendril embroidery patterns to trace the corner tendrils onto the appropriate corners of your quilt. Embroider the tendrils with a stem stitch and two strands of embroidery thread.

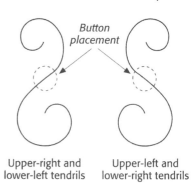

Button placement

Upper-right and lower-left tendrils

Upper-left and lower-right tendrils

Tendril embroidery patterns

COMPLETE THE ARRANGEMENT

Refer to "Finishing Your Quilt" (page 26).

1. Layer the quilt top with the batting and backing; baste.

2. Quilt as desired.

3. Square up the quilt top.

4. Add a rod pocket and bind the quilt using the 2" x 42" floral strips.

5. Add the buttons to the embroidered tendrils and stems.

6. Label the back of your quilt.

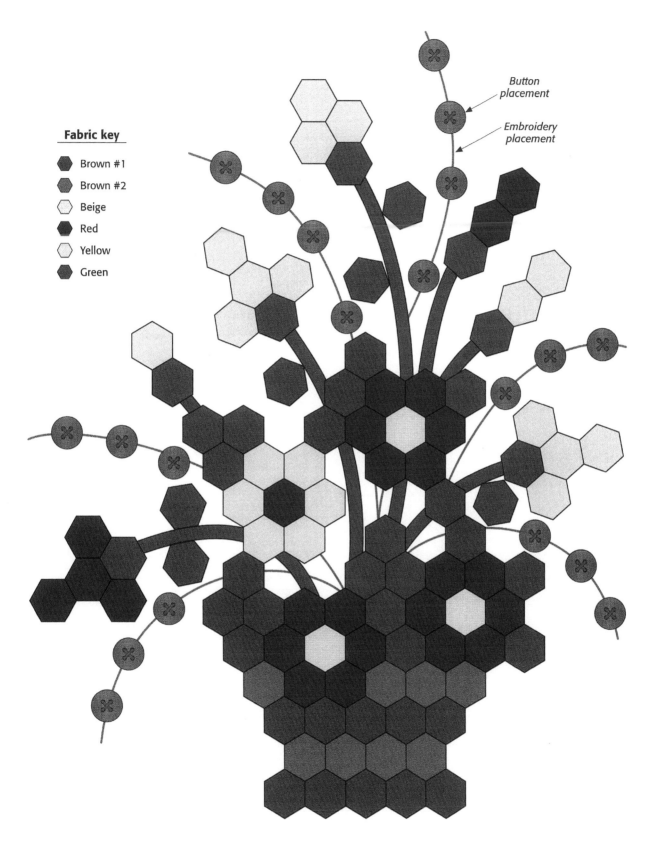

Fabric key

- Brown #1
- Brown #2
- Beige
- Red
- Yellow
- Green

Button placement

Embroidery placement

Floral arrangement layout diagram

Grandmother's Flower Garden

For those who love the traditional Grandmother's Flower Garden design,
this little quilt is just for you. It features a miniature quilt design in the center,
with potted flowers and vines intertwined around the edges. Create a
classic look and an updated floral arrangement—all in one great quilt!

MATERIALS

Yardage is based on 42"-wide fabric.

½ yard of dark green print for outer border, binding, and flower and leaf hexagons

¼ yard of cream print for flower hexagons

⅛ yard of brown print for inner border and planter

22" x 24" piece of cream tone-on-tone print for background

9" x 14" piece of red for flower and flower-center hexagons

9" x 14" piece of green-and-red print for flower hexagons

9" x 11" piece of brown floral print for flower hexagons

9" x 11" piece of green print for flower hexagons

8" x 8" piece *each* of light, medium, and dark green solids for appliqué leaves

⅔ yard for backing and rod pocket

24" x 27" piece of batting

Embroidery thread in dark green for stems and medium green for tendrils

20–25 buttons, ¼" diameter (or smaller), for berries

2 ladybug buttons and 1 bee button (or embellishments of your choice)

CUTTING

Cut the pieces listed below *before* cutting fabric for the hexagons.

From the brown print, cut:

● 2 strips, ⅝" x 42"; crosscut to make:
  2 strips, ⅝" x 15½"
  2 strips, ⅝" x 17¾"

From the dark green print, cut:

● 2 strips, 2½" x 42"; crosscut *each* strip to make:
  1 strip, 2½" x 15¾" (2 total)
  1 strip, 2½" x 21¾" (2 total)

● 2 strips, 2" x 42"

DESIGNER ALERT

Use this simple appliquéd flowerpot and leaves as a base for your own floral arrangement. Simply add your own combination of hexagon flowers, tendrils, and embellishments in the colors you desire. Consider using this design in a variety of ways, including the following:

● *Angled in each corner with the flowers and vines becoming the borders*

● *As a basket hung from an elaborate wrought-iron hanger*

● *As the floral centerpiece of a larger quilt*

● *Arranged all in a row like a windowsill of violet pots*

● *Stairstepped up or down, or randomly scattered about*

Make more than one arrangement so that you can change it with the seasons, holidays, and special events.

ASSEMBLE THE QUILT TOP

1. Refer to "English Paper Piecing Miniature Hexagons" (page 12) to prepare ¼" hexagons in the colors and quantities shown in the fabric key below. Use the basted hexagons to create the flower units in the quantities specified.

Make 1.

Make 2.

Make 1.

Make 1.

Unit A

Make 1.

Make 1.

Make 5.

Make 2.

Unit B

Make 1.

Make 1.

Make 2.

Make 3.

Unit C

Make 1.

Make 1.

Make 1.

Make 1.

Unit D

Fabric key

- ⬡ Red (77)
- ⬡ Brown floral print (67)
- ⬡ Green print (63)
- ⬡ Green-and-red print (75)
- ⬡ Dark green print (227)
- ⬡ Cream print (216)

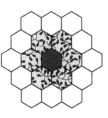
Make 2.

Make 1.

Unit E

Make 5.

Make 5.

Make 8.

Unit F

2. Join 196 of the dark green hexagons and the 18 flowers (the F units) in horizontal rows as shown in the row assembly diagrams.

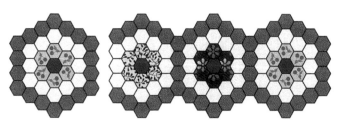
Assembly diagram for rows 1, 3, and 5.
Make 3.

Assembly diagram for rows 2 and 4.
Make 2.

3. Join the rows as shown in the assembly diagram.

Assembly diagram

DESIGNER ALERT
To reduce bulk after you've joined all the rows, remove all paper templates except those on the outer perimeter of your miniature quilt.

4. Enlarge the floral arrangement layout diagram on page 56 by 250% and use it as a pattern to baste the miniature quilt onto the cream tone-on-tone background rectangle, placing the quilt slightly toward the upper-left corner. Appliqué the quilt in place using matching thread.

5. Square up the background fabric to 15½" x 17½", being careful to keep the miniature quilt in the upper left, approximately 2" from the left side and 2" from the top edge.

6. Sew the ⅝" x 15½" brown print strips to the top and bottom of the background rectangle. Press the seam allowances toward the brown strips. Sew the ⅝" x 17¾" brown print strips to the sides of the rectangle. Press the seam allowances toward the brown strips.

7. Sew the 2½" x 15¾" dark green print strips to the top and bottom of the quilt top. Press the seam allowances toward the green strips. Sew the 2½" x 21¾" dark green print strips to the sides of the quilt top. Press the seam allowances toward the green strips.

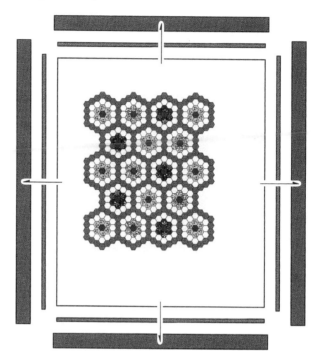

8. Use your enlarged floral arrangement layout diagram as a pattern to lightly trace the stems, tendrils, flowers, leaves, and planter onto the background fabric.

9. Embroider the stems and tendrils in place. Use six strands of thread and a chain stitch for the stems and two strands of thread and a stem stitch for the tendrils. (See "Embroidery Stitches" on page 22.)

10. Using the templates (page 57), cut out 10 large and 16 small vine leaves, the planter base and rim, and the planter leaves.

11. Baste the flower units and the partial hexagon border in place in this order: planter base, planter rim, planter leaves (in the order specified on the templates), flowers, vine leaves, and the partial hexagonal border in the upper-left corner. Appliqué the units in place with matching thread.

Embroidery
placement

Button
placement

Floral arrangement layout diagram
Enlarge 250%.

Fabric key

⬢ Red	⬢ Green-and-red print	⬬ Light green
⬢ Brown floral print	⬢ Dark green print	⬬ Medium green
⬢ Green print	⬡ Cream print	⬬ Dark green solid

COMPLETE THE ARRANGEMENT

Refer to "Finishing Your Quilt" (page 26).

1. Layer the quilt top with the batting and backing; baste.

2. Quilt as desired.

3. Square up the quilt top.

4. Add a rod pocket and bind the quilt using the 2" x 42" dark green print strips.

5. Add the berry buttons and any additional button embellishments desired. I added two ladybug buttons on leaves, as well as a bee pin buzzing across the background above the miniature quilt.

6. Label the back of your quilt.

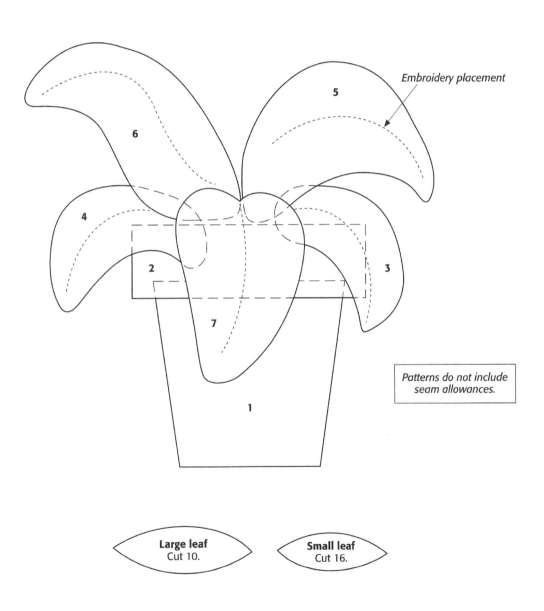

Embroidery placement

Patterns do not include
seam allowances.

Large leaf
Cut 10.

Small leaf
Cut 16.

Sunflower Bouquet

Nothing makes me smile more than a field full of sunflowers—
when I see these beautiful blooms, my day suddenly becomes sunny
and bright! Make this simple wall quilt to bring that same feeling into
your home every day. You're sure to smile every time you see it.

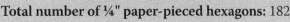
MATERIALS

Yardage is based on 42"-wide fabric.

⅓ yard of brown-and-green print for outer border

⅓ yard of brown tone-on-tone print for inner border, binding, and vase-trim hexagons

¼ yard of beige print for outer-border corner squares and vase hexagons

⅛ yard of sunny yellow for middle border and sunflower-petal hexagons

12" x 22" piece of green tone-on-tone print for background

5" x 9" piece of pale yellow for sunflower-petal hexagons

5" x 9" piece or scraps of dark brown for sunflower-center hexagons

5" x 8" piece of dark green for leaves

5" x 8" piece of medium green for leaves

2" x 9" piece of green for flower-bud hexagons

⅔ yard for backing and rod pocket

24" x 32" piece of batting

Embroidery thread in medium green for flower stems

CUTTING

Cut the pieces listed below *before* cutting fabric for the hexagons.

From the brown tone-on-tone print, cut:

- 2 strips, 1½" x 42"; crosscut to make:
  2 strips, 1½" x 12"
  2 strips, 1½" x 17½"
- 3 strips, 2" x 42"

From the sunny yellow, cut:

- 2 strips, ¾" x 42"; crosscut to make:
  2 strips, ¾" x 12½"
  2 strips, ¾" x 19½"

From the brown-and-green print, cut:

- 2 strips, 4½" x 42"; crosscut to make:
  2 strips, 4½" x 12½"
  2 strips, 4½" x 20"

From the beige print, cut:

- 4 squares, 6" x 6"

ASSEMBLE THE QUILT TOP

1. Refer to "English Paper Piecing Miniature Hexagons" (page 12) to prepare ¼" hexagons in the colors and quantities shown in the fabric key at left. Use the basted hexagons to create the flower units in the quantities specified.

Fabric key

- Dark brown (30)
- Green (7)
- Brown tone-on-tone (14)
- Beige (40)
- Sunny yellow (61)
- Pale yellow (30)

Make 2.

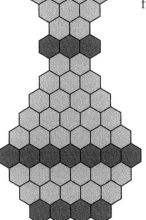
Make 1.

Make 7.

Make 6.

Make 1.

2. Use the templates (page 61) to make 17 dark green and 15 medium green leaves in the sizes indicated. Prepare the leaves for appliqué or fusing. (See "Fusing for Easier Appliqué" on page 19.)

DESIGNER ALERT

I made my leaves from Ultrasuede and fused them to the quilt before machine straight stitching ⅟₁₆" to ⅛" inside the leaf edges to permanently attach them.

3. Enlarge the floral arrangement layout diagram on page 61 by 200% and use it as a pattern to lightly trace the stem lines, leaf placement, and flower and vase locations onto the background fabric. Use the border corner layout diagrams to lightly trace the floral stem lines, leaf placement, and flower locations onto the 6" beige squares.

4. Embroider the flower stems in place using a stem stitch and six strands of medium green embroidery thread. (See "Stem Stitch" on page 24.)

5. Baste the central floral units and vase in place on the green tone-on-tone background rectangle; then baste the floral units to the outer-border corner squares. Appliqué the pieces in place using matching thread. Remove the basting stitches and paper templates.

6. Temporarily fuse or baste the leaves in place. Permanently attach the leaves using the basic blanket stitch, hand appliqué, or machine outline stitching. (See "Embroidery Stitches" on page 22.)

7. Square up the background rectangle to 10" x 17½", being careful to keep the arrangement in the center of the fabric. Square up the outer-border corner squares to 4½" x 4½".

8. Sew the 1½" x 17½" brown tone-on-tone strips to the sides of the background rectangle. Press the seam allowances toward the brown strips. Sew the 1½" x 12" brown tone-on-tone strips to the top and bottom of the background rectangle. Press the seam allowances toward the brown strips.

9. Sew the ¾" x 19½" sunny yellow strips to the sides of the quilt top. Press the seam allowances toward the yellow strips. Sew the ¾" x 12½" sunny yellow strips to the top and bottom edges of the quilt

top. Press the seam allowances toward the yellow strips.

10. Sew the 4½" x 20" brown-and-green print strips to the sides of the quilt top. Press the seam allowances toward the brown-and-green strips. Sew 4½" beige print squares to the ends of the 4½" x 12½" brown-and-green print strips, referring to the photo (page 58) to position the appliquéd flowers correctly. Press the seam allowances away from the corner squares. Sew the pieced strips to the top and bottom edges of the quilt. Press the seam allowances toward the brown-and-green strips.

COMPLETE THE ARRANGEMENT

Refer to "Finishing Your Quilt" (page 26).

1. Layer the quilt top with the batting and backing; baste.

2. Quilt as desired.

3. Square up the quilt top.

4. Add a rod pocket and bind the quilt using the 2" x 42" brown tone-on-tone strips.

5. Label the back of your quilt.

Fabric key

◆ Dark brown

◆ Green

⬡ Brown tone-on-tone

⬡ Beige

⬡ Sunny yellow

⬡ Pale yellow

🌰 Dark green

🌰 Medium green

Large leaf
Cut 12 dark green
and 11 medium green.

Small leaf
Cut 5 dark green
and 4 medium green.

*Patterns do not include
seam allowances.*

Floral arrangement layout diagram
Enlarge 200%.

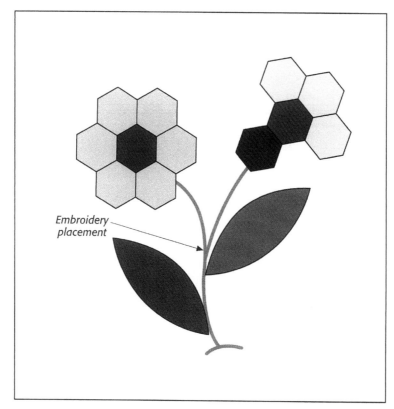

Embroidery
placement

Upper- and lower-left corners

Fabric key

⬡ Dark brown
⬡ Green
⬡ Brown tone-on-tone
⬡ Beige
⬡ Sunny yellow
⬡ Pale yellow
⬬ Dark green
⬬ Medium green

Upper- and lower-right corners

Floral arrangement layout diagrams

Topiary Rose

Bring an air of formality to your walls with this floral topiary-rose planter and border. If the bold summer colors of yellow and pink don't fit your décor, choose fall colors of orange and rust, Christmas colors of bright reds and greens, or whatever suits your taste. This floral arrangement will add beauty wherever it's displayed.

MATERIALS

Yardage is based on 42"-wide fabric.

½ yard of bright blue for background and wide inner border

⅓ yard of dark green print for outer border and binding

¼ yard of medium green print for narrow inner borders and leaf hexagons

⅛ yard of dark green for bias stems and topiary plant-stem hexagons

5" x 9" piece of dark pink for flower hexagons

5" x 9" piece of pink polka dot for flower hexagons

4" x 9" piece of brown print for planter-base hexagons

3" x 9" piece of medium pink for flower hexagons

3" x 9" piece of light pink for flower hexagons

3" x 9" piece of dark brown print for planter-rim hexagons

3" x 9" piece of bright gold for flower-center hexagons

½ yard for backing and rod pocket

18" x 24" piece of batting

CUTTING

Cut the pieces listed below *before* cutting fabric for the hexagons.

From the bright blue, cut:

- 2 strips, 2" x 42"; crosscut to make:
  2 strips, 2" x 12¾"
  2 strips, 2" x 10"
- 1 rectangle, 10" x 16"

From the medium green print, cut:

- 3 strips, ¾" x 42"; crosscut to make:
  2 strips, ¾" x 12¼"
  2 strips, ¾" x 7"
  2 strips, ¾" x 15¾"
  2 strips, ¾" x 10½"

From the dark green print, cut:

- 2 strips, 2½" x 42"; crosscut to make:
  2 strips, 2½" x 16¼"
  2 strips, 2½" x 14½"
- 2 strips, 2" x 42"

ASSEMBLE THE QUILT TOP

1. Refer to "English Paper Piecing Miniature Hexagons" (page 12) to prepare ¼" hexagons in the colors and quantities shown in the fabric key on the facing page. Use the basted hexagons to create the flower units in the quantities specified.

2. Refer to the floral arrangement layout diagram on page 66 to sew all the center topiary-rose parts together as one unit.

3. Make 16 bias stems, each about 2" long. (Refer to "Making ⅛" Bias Stems" on page 18.)

4. Enlarge the floral arrangement layout diagram by 200% and use it as a pattern to lightly trace the stem lines, planter, flowers, and leaf locations onto the 10" x 16" bright blue background rectangle.

5. Baste the center topiary unit in place. Appliqué the shape using matching thread. Remove the basting stitches and paper templates.

6. Square up the background fabric to 6½" x 12¼", being careful to center the topiary.

7. Sew the ¾" x 12¼" medium green print strips to the sides of the background rectangle. Press the seam allowances toward the green strips. Sew the ¾" x 7" medium green print strips to the top and bottom of the rectangle. Press the seam allowances toward the green strips.

8. Sew the 2" x 12¾" bright blue strips to the sides of the quilt top. Press the seam allowances toward the blue strips. Sew the 2" x 10" bright blue strips to the top and bottom of the quilt top. Press the seam allowances toward the blue strips.

9. Sew the ¾" x 15¾" medium green print strips to the sides of the quilt top. Press the seam allowances toward the green strips. Sew the ¾" x 10½"

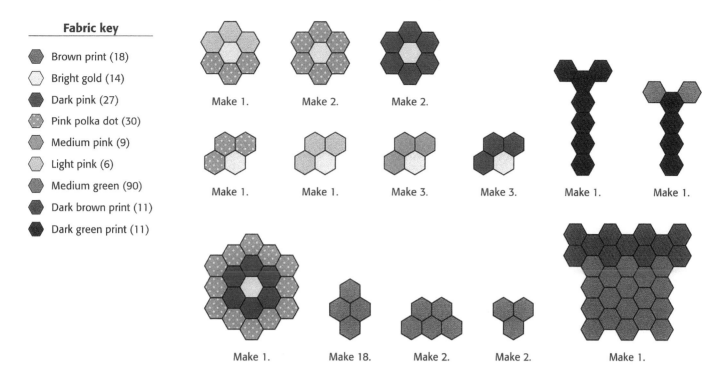

Make 1. Make 2. Make 2.

Make 1. Make 1. Make 3. Make 3. Make 1. Make 1.

Make 1. Make 18. Make 2. Make 2. Make 1.

medium green print strips to the top and bottom of the quilt top. Press the seam allowances toward the green strips.

10. Sew the 2½" x 16¼" dark green print strips to the sides of the quilt top. Press the seam allowances toward the green strips. Sew the 2½" x 14½" dark green print strips to the top and bottom of the quilt top. Press the seam allowances toward the green strips.

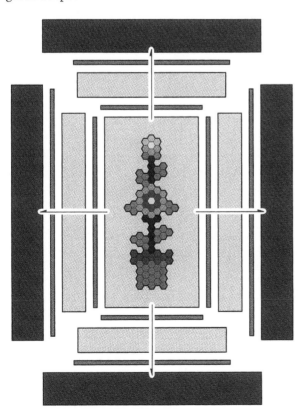

11. Using your enlarged floral arrangement layout diagram, lightly trace the bias-stem lines, leaf placement, and flower locations for the appliqué border onto the bright blue border. Be careful to keep your stems centered within the border. Baste and then appliqué the bias-stem segments in place using matching thread.

12. Baste each of the floral units in place, making sure the bias-stem ends are tucked under the leaf and flower units. Appliqué using matching thread. Remove the basting stitches and paper templates.

COMPLETE THE ARRANGEMENT

Refer to "Finishing Your Quilt" (page 26).

1. Layer the quilt top with the batting and backing; baste.

2. Quilt as desired.

3. Square up the quilt top.

4. Add a rod pocket and bind the quilt using the 2" x 42" dark green print strips.

5. Label the back of your quilt.

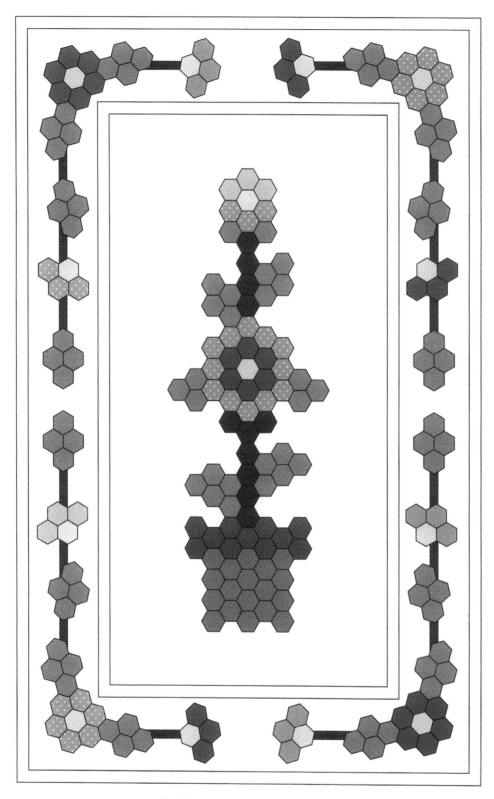

Fabric key

- Brown print
- Bright gold
- Dark pink
- Pink polka dot
- Medium pink
- Light pink
- Medium green
- Dark brown print
- Dark green print

Floral arrangement layout diagram
Enlarge 200%.

Welcome Home

Let this wall quilt send a friendly message to family and friends as they enter your home.
Make it in colors that evoke a specific holiday or season, such as Thanksgiving or Christmas,
or select your fabrics and colors with that one special person in mind whose homecoming
is a special event. Whatever the color palette, the message will truly warm hearts.

FINISHED QUILT: 24½" x 28½"
Total number of ½" paper-pieced hexagons: 52

MATERIALS

Yardage is based on 42"-wide fabric.

⅓ yard of light brown print for outer border

⅓ yard of dark brown print for inner border, binding, and flower hexagons

¼ yard of medium brown print for middle border, outer-border corner squares, and flower hexagons

18" x 22" piece (fat quarter) of cream print for background

8" x 8" piece of dark brown for letters

6" x 9" piece of dark green solid for leaves

6" x 9" piece of medium green solid for leaves

6" x 9" piece of large floral print for flower and flower-center hexagons

6" x 9" piece of dark gold for flower hexagons

2" x 9" piece of medium green print for flower-base hexagons

30" x 42" piece for backing and rod pocket

30" x 36" piece of batting

Embroidery thread in green for stems

CUTTING

Cut the pieces listed below *before* cutting fabric for the hexagons.

From the dark brown print, cut:

● 2 strips, 1½" x 42"; crosscut to make:
   2 strips, 1½" x 14½"
   2 strips, 1½" x 20½"
● 3 strips, 2" x 42"

From the medium brown print, cut:

● 2 strips, 1" x 42"; crosscut to make:
   2 strips, 1" x 16½"
   2 strips, 1" x 21½"
● 4 squares, 4" x 4"

From the light brown print, cut:

● 2 strips, 4" x 42"; crosscut to make:
   2 strips, 4" x 17½"
   2 strips, 4" x 21½"

ASSEMBLE THE QUILT TOP

1. Refer to "English Paper Piecing Miniature Hexagons" (page 12) to prepare ½" hexagons in the colors and quantities shown in the fabric key below. Use the basted hexagons to create the flower units in the quantities specified.

2. Use the template at the bottom of the page to make 10 leaves from the medium green solid

Fabric key

● Dark brown (11)

● Medium brown (11)

● Floral (10)

● Dark gold (12)

● Medium green print (8)

Make 1.

Make 1.

Make 1.

Make 1.

Make 2.

Make 4.

Make 1.

Make 1.

and 8 leaves from the dark green solid. Prepare them for whatever method of appliqué you prefer. (See "Fusing for Easier Appliqué" on page 19.)

DESIGNER ALERT

I used felted wool for the leaves and Ultrasuede for the letters.

3. Enlarge the floral arrangement layout diagram on page 70 by 200% and use it as a pattern to lightly trace the stem lines, leaf, and flower locations onto the 18" x 22" cream print background rectangle.

4. Use the stem stitch and six strands of green embroidery thread to embroider the flower stems in place. (See "Stem Stitch" on page 24.)

5. Baste the flower units and leaves in place, with the exception of the two floral units and two leaves that overlap the inner border. (These four appliqués will need to be added *after* the borders have been sewn on.) Appliqué the units in place using matching thread. Remove the basting stitches and paper templates.

6. Square up the background rectangle to 14½" x 18½", positioning the floral arrangement in the lower-right corner.

7. Sew the 1½" x 14½" dark brown print strips to the top and bottom edges of the background rectangle. Press the seam allowances toward the brown strips. Sew the 1½" x 20½" dark brown print strips to the sides of the background rectangle. Press the seam allowances toward the brown strips.

8. Sew the 1" x 16½" medium brown print strips to the top and bottom edges of the quilt top. Press the seam allowances toward the medium brown strips. Sew the 1" x 21½" medium brown print strips to the sides of the quilt top. Press the seam allowances toward the medium brown strips.

9. Sew the 4" x 17½" light brown print strips to the top and bottom edges of the quilt top. Press seam allowances toward the light brown strips. Sew a 4" medium brown print square to each end of the 4" x 21½" light brown print strips. Press the seam allowances away from the corner squares. Stitch the pieced strips to the sides of the quilt top. Press the seam allowances toward the light brown strips.

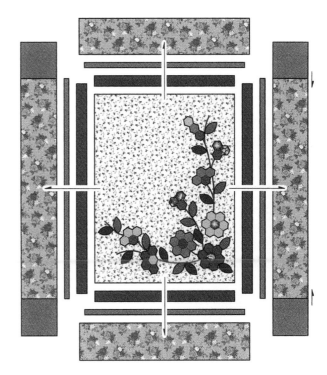

10. Baste and appliqué the remaining flowers and leaves in place, overlapping the inner border.

11. Use your enlarged floral arrangement layout diagram to prepare and appliqué the letters by machine or hand. (You could also create your own message with the letters on page 77.) Position your message in the upper-left quadrant of your background fabric. (Refer to "Block Letters" on page 24 and "Fusing for Easier Appliqué" on page 19 as needed.)

COMPLETE THE ARRANGEMENT

Refer to "Finishing Your Quilt" (page 26).

1. Layer the quilt top with the batting and backing; baste.

2. Quilt as desired.

3. Square up the quilt top.

4. Add a rod pocket and bind the quilt using the 2" x 42" dark brown print strips.

5. Label the back of your quilt.

Leaf
Cut 8 dark green
and 10 medium green.

*Pattern does not include
seam allowance.*

Fabric key

- Dark brown
- Medium brown
- Floral
- Dark gold
- Medium green print
- Medium green solid
- Dark green

WELCOME
HOME

Floral arrangement layout diagram
Enlarge 200%.

Wreath for All Seasons

Let this beautiful wreath grace your mantle or entrance hall during the holidays—
or even after. Create it, as I have, in the reds, greens, and golds of Christmas,
or make it shout "Spring is here!" in yellows and pinks. Better yet, create
one for each season, using warm orange, brown, and gold tones for
autumn and bright reds, yellows, and blues for summer.

MATERIALS

Yardage is based on 42"-wide fabric.

⅛ yard *each* or scraps of 8–10 assorted green fabrics for wreath hexagons

36" x 36" piece of cream print for background

⅔ yard of red striped fabric for outer border

⅝ yard of red print #1 for inner border and binding

½ yard of gold print for middle border and bow hexagons

¼ yard of medium green print for border corner squares and wreath hexagons

9" x 13" piece of red print #2 for flower hexagons

9" x 13" piece of red print #3 for flower hexagons

7" x 9" piece of red print #4 for flower hexagons

2" x 9" piece *each* of 2 assorted floral fabrics for flower-center hexagons

2" x 9" piece of red print #5 for flower hexagons

2" x 9" piece of red print #6 for flower hexagons

2¾ yards for backing and rod pocket

50" x 50" piece of batting

Approximately 26 small jingle bells or other desired embellishments

DESIGNER ALERT
For my flower centers, I fussy cut the centers of printed fabric flowers. This gives the wreath added texture and a realistic touch.

CUTTING

Cut the pieces listed below *before* cutting fabric for the hexagons.

From red print #1, cut:

● 4 strips, 1½" x 42"; crosscut to make:
   4 strips, 1½" x 29"
● 5 strips, 2" x 42"

From the gold, cut:

● 4 strips, 2½" x 42"; crosscut to make:
   4 strips, 2½" x 31"

From the red striped fabric, cut:

● 4 strips, 5½" x 42"; crosscut to make:
   4 strips, 5½" x 35"

From the medium green print, cut:

● 4 squares, 1½" x 1½"
● 4 squares, 2½" x 2½"
● 4 squares, 5½" x 5½"

ASSEMBLE THE QUILT TOP

1. Refer to "English Paper Piecing Miniature Hexagons" (page 12) to prepare ½" hexagons in the colors and quantities shown in the fabric key below. Use the basted hexagons to construct the four sections of the wreath.

2. Join the four sections as shown in the layout diagram.

3. Remove all the basting stitches and paper templates from the surrounded hexagons only—leave the templates in the hexagons on the outer edges.

4. Baste the wreath in the center of the 36" x 36" cream print square. Appliqué it in place using your desired method and matching thread.

5. Remove the remaining basting stitches and paper templates from the edges of the wreath. Press.

6. Square up the background piece to 29" x 29".

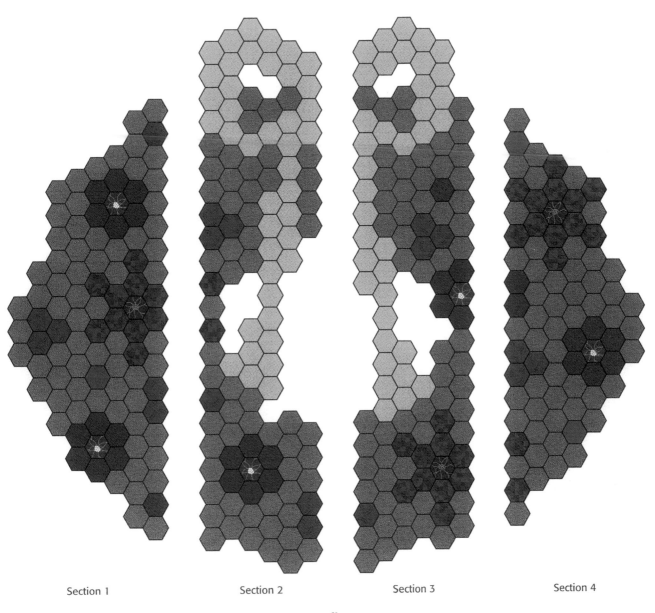

Section 1   Section 2   Section 3   Section 4

Layout diagram

Fabric key		
⬡ Gold print (78)	⬡ Red print #2 (36)	⬡ Red print #5 (3)
⬡ Floral #1 (5)	⬡ Red print #3 (30)	⬡ Red print #6 (3)
⬡ Floral #2 (3)	⬡ Red print #4 (18)	⬡ Assorted greens (233)

7. Sew 1½" x 29" red print #1 strips to the sides of the center square. Press the seam allowances toward the red strips. Sew a 1½" x 1½" medium green square to each end of the remaining 1½" x 29" red print #1 strips. Press the seam allowances away from the squares. Sew the pieced strips to the top and bottom of the center square. Press the seam allowances toward the red strips.

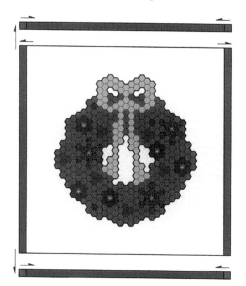

8. Sew 2½" x 31" gold print strips to the sides of the quilt top. Press the seam allowances toward the gold strips. Sew a 2½" x 2½" medium green square to each end of the remaining gold strips. Press the seam allowances away from the squares. Sew the pieced strips to the top and bottom of the quilt top. Press the seam allowances toward the gold strips.

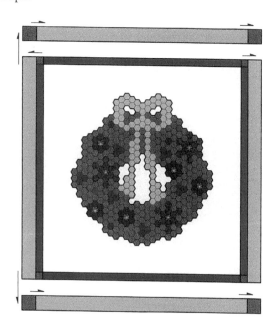

9. Sew 5½" x 35" red striped strips to the sides of the quilt top. Press the seam allowances toward the red striped fabric. Sew a 5½" x 5½" medium green square to each end of the remaining red striped strips. Press the seam allowances away from the squares. Sew the pieced strips to the top and bottom of the quilt top. Press the seam allowances toward the red strips.

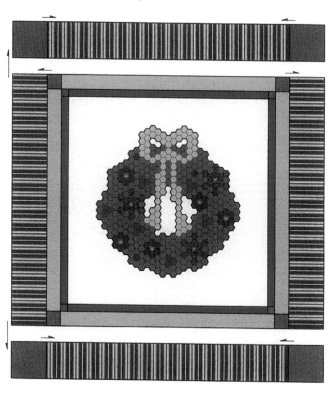

COMPLETE THE ARRANGEMENT

Refer to "Finishing Your Quilt" (page 26).

1. Layer the quilt top with the batting and backing; baste.

2. Quilt as desired.

3. Square up the quilt top.

4. Add a rod pocket and bind the quilt using the 2" x 42" red print #1 strips.

5. Add the jingle bells or other desired embellishments. Beads, buttons, and bells would all work on this project.

6. Label the back of your quilt.

Floral-Unit Assembly Diagrams

Use the units shown here to modify the projects in this book or to create your own original fabric floral arrangements. Use hexagonal graph paper, available at art-supply stores, to experiment with these units and your own designs.

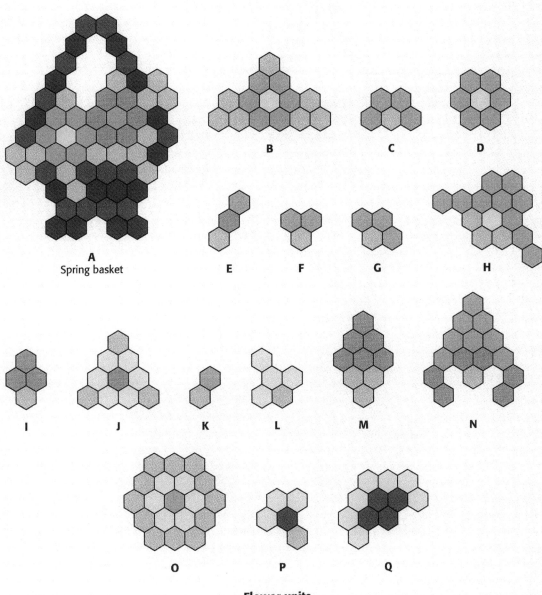

A
Spring basket

B

C

D

E

F

G

H

I

J

K

L

M

N

O

P

Q

Flower units

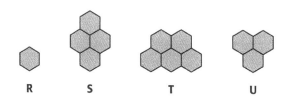

Leaves and foliage

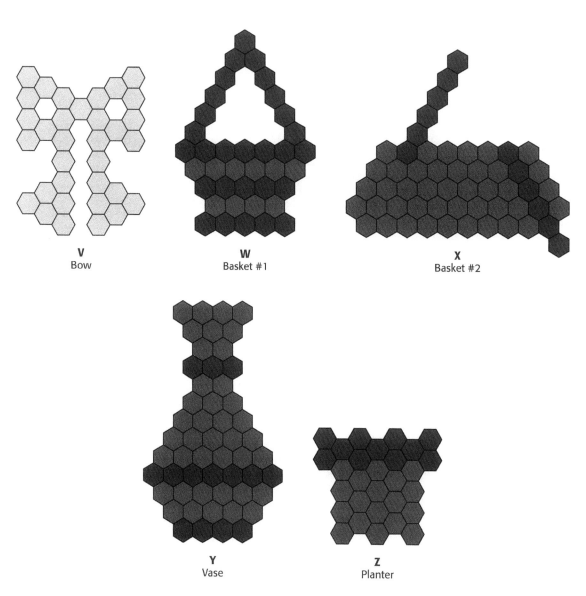

V
Bow

W
Basket #1

X
Basket #2

Y
Vase

Z
Planter

Containers and accessories

Alphabets and Numbers

ABCDEFG
HIJKLMN
OPQRSTU
VWXYZ12
34567890

Block characters

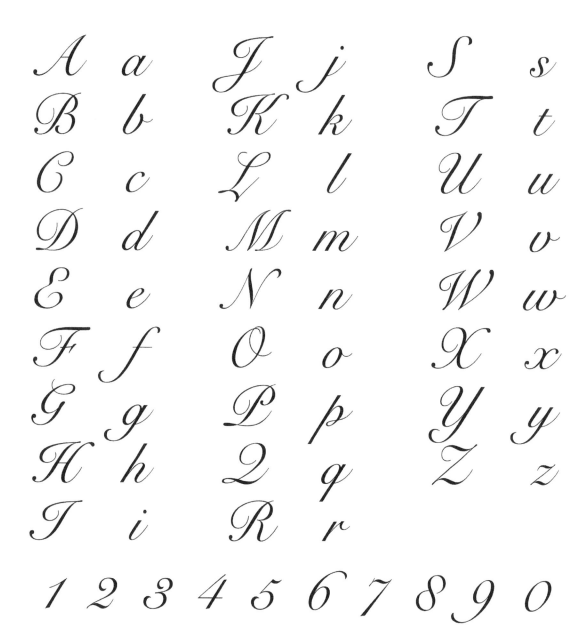

Script characters

Resources

For ¼" and ½" precut hexagon-template foundations:
Paper Pieces
PO Box 68
Sycamore, IL 60178
Phone: 1-800-337-1537
Fax: 1-815-899-2900
Web site: www.paperpieces.com

For Ultrasuede:
Ultra Delight
Leota Black
PO Box 51108
Amarillo, TX 79159
Phone: 1-806-351-0508
Email: lblack@centramedia.net

About the Author

Jaynette Huff lives in Conway, Arkansas, with her husband, Larry, and their cat and dog, Inky and Buddy.

This is Jaynette's fourth book with Martingale & Company and her first on English paper piecing. Her first three books, including *Christmas Delights* (2003), were all on foundation piecing.

Jaynette's interest in English paper piecing grew from her love of miniature quiltmaking. Attempting to make miniature quilts using a variety of design types and techniques, she decided to try a miniature Grandmother's Flower Garden quilt, but using ¼" hexagons. She was hooked! One hexagon quilt followed another—even one using ⅛" hexagons!

Jaynette has discovered that the world of miniature quiltmaking is an ever-expanding adventure for her—new designs, new techniques, new products. She has also found it to be extremely fulfilling, and she enjoys sharing the adventure with other quilters and friends.

CPSIA information can be obtained
at www.ICGtesting.com
Printed in the USA
LVIW011427090512

281062LV00007B